ONE

''Scuse me, d'you know where David Bowie lives?'

THE CRY OF YOUNG PILGRIMS lost in a land beyond London's postcodes, where the banging clanging city finally yawns itself to sleep in suburban Kent. Conspicuous strangers with paintbox faces, some boys, some girls, some shy blushered creatures less obviously either, but every one adoring Magi guided by the same star twinkling in any number of pop weeklies.

'At his art nouveau decorated house in Beckenham . . .'

'His home in Beckenham reflects his artistic tastes . . .'

'His rambling Victorian mansion in Beckenham . . .'

Beckenham?

A name and a place that means nothing to heads full of crisps and Clearasil and Radio Luxembourg until the moment they learn *that's* where David Bowie lives.

'His home . . .'

Adolescent senses prick like sharks to the smell of distant blood.

'. . . in Beckenham.'

Hungry eyes gorge on timetables and departure boards.

BECKENHAM!

Thirty minutes on a train out of Charing Cross or any number of buses serving Croydon, Lewisham, Woolwich and Crystal Palace. Which for the kids living in and around the capital means Shangri-La is there on their doorstep for a mere cheap day return.

'Two to Beckenham Junction, please!'

Here comes another pair now, wandering out of the station, over made-up faces beaming with the guiltless thrill of truancy, both in brightly coloured tights and chunky clogs poking out beneath the dull yet practical coats this see-your-breath January day demands. As happy to be where they want to be as they are clueless as where to go next.

What did they expect? A flashing neon sign with a pointing finger: 'DAVID BOWIE'S HOUSE THIS WAY'?

Instead, a half-empty station car park opposite Twiggs Motors car showroom. To the left, a driving school ending a small row of shops by the railway bridge. To the right, more shops opposite a large stretch of green. They stand and twitch and chew their fingernails.

Eeny, meeny, miny . . .

And on they moe, sloping down the hill to a provincial town refusing to surrender its horse and cart daydreams of being a country village. One windy main street of oak-beamed pubs, striped shop awnings, slow bicyclists and bloomless flower beds: a perfect snow globe Little England with its garage, hairdresser, butcher, fishmonger, ironmonger, newsagent, greengrocer, a Wimpy bar, a Sainsbury's, a Boots and one ABC cinema playing two-month catch-up with the West End. But nowhere do they see anything resembling a '*rambling Victorian mansion*'.

The pilgrims clop on, sniggering, pointing, clutching at each other's arms, exciting each other that they might see *him* at any moment: in every shop window, across the street, in every passing car, at every traffic light. Even if the more of Beckenham they see, the more it feels like trying to find Ziggy Stardust on the streets of Chigley. That's when the 'scusing starts.

''Scuse me, d'you know where David Bowie lives?'

Everyone they ask might as well be 100 years old. Plump harassed mothers pushing blue murder prams.

'Sorry, darling.'

Opening-time drunks with faces like a stubbed-out Senior Service.

'Eh, schweetheart?'

Headscarfed housewives rattling tins of Whiskas in wicker shopping baskets.

BOWIEODYSSEY73

Also by Simon Goddard

Bowie Odyssey 72
Bowie Odyssey 71
Bowie Odyssey 70
The Comeback
Rollaresque
Simply Thrilled
Ziggyology
Mozipedia
Songs That Saved Your Life

BOWIE ODYSSEY 73

SIMON GODDARD

OMNIBUS PRESS

London / New York / Paris / Sydney / Copenhagen / Berlin / Madrid / Tokyo

Note to the Reader: The following narrative takes place in 1973 and contains language and prevailing attitudes of the time which some readers may find offensive. The publishers wish to reassure that all such instances are there specifically for reasons of historical social context in order to accurately describe the period concerned.

Copyright © 2023 Omnibus Press
(A division of the Wise Music Group
14–15 Berners Street, London, W1T 3LJ)

Paperback cover image and endpapers by Masayoshi Sukita
Hardback cover image by Shutterstock
Cover designed by Fabrice Couillerot
Picture research by Simon Goddard

Paperback ISBN 978-1-9131-7281-7
Hardback ISBN 978-1-9131-7282-4

A catalogue record for this book is available from the British Library.

Typeset by Evolution Design & Digital Ltd (Kent)
Printed in Malta

www.omnibuspress.com

BOWIECONTENTS73

'My most trendy teenage friend tells me that to call someone decadent is the biggest compliment you can pay them. What did she mean by the word, I asked. She said she didn't know but David Bowie was decadent.'

JILLY COOPER,
THE SUNDAY TIMES,
JULY 1973

What disease would you most like for the New Year?
a.   Anal syphilis from a bar-room queen in Memphis.
b.   Coming over all funny.
c.   Back surgery from the Ogre of Sacramento.
d.   Collapsed nostrils.

'THE DECADENCE QUIZ',
TIME OUT,
DECEMBER 1973

'Who's that, dear?'

All of them uncaring adult monsters, zombified by Anadin, Cinzano Bianco, *Z-Cars* and the scandalous rise in the cost of a Sunday joint.

'Cos me husband likes beef but I will not pay for it in gold bars!'

How can they not *know* David Bowie when they live *here*, in his home, breathing the same precious air? Don't they watch *Top of the Pops*? Didn't they *see* him on it last week making hot harmonica sex of 'The Jean Genie' with his gorgeous copper hair and his lickable cheekbones and his jacket so lustrous the TV screen couldn't even keep up with its mercurial silvery bluey gold shimmer? Don't they *read* magazines? Don't they *listen* to the radio? Don't they *buy* . . .

RECORDS

The sign stops them dead in their tracks like an Angel of the Lord. Gleaming below the swirly lettering of an electrical goods store, Robertson's, its windows advertising televisions, refrigerators, stereos and . . .

'Records!'

They clatter through the double doors, ignoring price-slashed washing machines, tripping up the stairs following the arrows to the music department. It is empty save for the background rasp of Rod Stewart and one rather bored salesgirl fiddling with a sticker gun behind the counter. Beside her, a wall rack where the fists and thumbs of Slade proudly poke out from the cover of *Slayed?* She *must* know.

'. . . where David Bowie lives?'

The salesgirl blinks as if suddenly awoken from a trance. Staring back at her are two heavily mascaraed innocents drunk with the prospect of corruption. She pokes a coy tongue in her cheek, eyes darting around the shopfloor as if making sure no clip-tied boss is in earshot.

'Yeah,' she says cautiously. 'Actually, we get a lot of his fans coming in here.' Her eyes flit between them as a sly smirk emerges. 'Shouldn't you two be in school?

'Aw, please! We've come all the way from Ruislip!'

The assistant screws her mouth to one side, hums a ponderous 'hmm', hands idly picking at her sticker roll. Then puts them out of their misery.

'Oh, OK.'

The pilgrims shake.

'But don't you *dare* tell anyone I told you,' she adds, wagging a finger.

'No, we won't! Promise!'

'How'd you get here? By train?'

'Yes!'

'Well,' she lowers her voice, drawing their heads in over the counter towards her, 'you need to go back up the hill the way you came, past the station and keep going over the bridge. Just keep following Southend Road. Carry on along it all the way up and eventually you'll come to his house on the right.'

'How will we know?'

'You'll know it when you see it.'

'Southend?'

'Road, yes.'

'Aw, you're smashing! Thanks!'

'I never told you, *remember*?'

'Yes, yes, we won't tell, promise! Thanks! Bye! Thanks so much! Bye! Thanks! Thanks! Thanks!'

Clogs clatter down the stairs, out the doors, back up the high street, every shop, pedestrian and paving stone now just a blur, seeing nothing and no one, hearts beating, breath steaming, passing the station, gasping at the sign for 'SOUTHEND ROAD', clatter, clatter, clatter, not caring what cars nearly run them over at the crossroads with The Avenue, clop, clop, clop as the shops vanish, and the pavements get quieter, and the trees get bigger, and the houses slowly stretch further apart, and the road gets longer, and they start to panic, and 'Wot if we've missed it?', and the clattering slows, and 'Maybe we should go back?', and 'She said you can't miss it!', and 'Is that one his house?', and 'How should I know!', and 'Just keep going a bit further', and 'Who are them kids up there?', and suddenly clogged-feet freeze and 'OH MY GOD!'

A rambling Victorian mansion.

It lurks back from the main road like a Gothic castle, moated by its own driveway curving through an ornate front garden of bushes and shrubs. Stone steps lead up to a porch dripping with ivy where the name 'HADDON HALL' hangs down from the arched entrance. Either side of it jut large bay windows, upstairs and downstairs, while above it a large square turret thrusts upwards through the roof like a launching rocket. It is old and spooky and not remotely rockstarish, and if it wasn't for the scratched and scribbled 'ZIGGY's on and around the steps where five other pilgrims are already loitering they might never believe they've reached the right place. But they have.

This is where David Bowie lives.

'We ain't seen him yet today.' The greeting of a delicate-faced boy in a parka with a *Space Oddity* LP tucked under his arm. 'Don't think he's in.'

The girls creep nervously towards them, eyes ping-ponging from window to window, desperate for any brief flash of red hair or spangly cloth. 'Which one's his bedroom?' they ask and an older girl in a purple suede coat tells them he lives on the bottom floor. 'The rest of it's different flats,' says another. 'We've met some of his neighbours. Some's quite nice. Most of 'em ignore us, apart from this old man wot comes round sometimes. Must be the landlord or sumfink as he's always telling us to get lost or he'll call the Old Bill.'

The pilgrims listen in reverent awe to tales of ringing the bell and speaking to his wife, of being brought cups of tea and biscuits, of the time she lost her patience and yelled 'FUCK OFF!', the number of times they've actually seen *him* coming and going, of the fabulous clothes he wears, never in the same stitch twice, and the warm friendly waves he gives them from the back of his limousine. As, all the while, the ancient house holds its breath in deathly silence. Not a peep, not a stir, not a curtain twitch. Nothing moves, not even time.

Until the fading winter daylight threatens to smother them. The skies darken fast as their resignation. The pilgrims tighten their coats. Home is one train, one Tube, one missed tea and a serious parental bollocking away. They take a longing last look at his strange old house.

'Wait,' says one, suddenly rummaging in her inside pocket. 'We can't go without letting him know we've been. Ain't got a pen, 'ave ya?'

'No.'

'. . . hang about, then . . .'

'Come on, Brend! We'll miss our train!'

''S'alright, this'll do!'

She pulls out the 'Strawberry Fool' she got for Christmas, unscrewing its soft waxy tip. Then, crouching on her knees by the steps, she slowly and carefully starts to write the name of David Bowie. As big and bold as she can, pressing hard with thick red lipstick . . .

THICK RED LIPSTICK presses hard upon the face of David Bowie. His forehead, his nose, his cheek, everywhere except his actual lips.

Ten miles as the crow flies from his graffitied front step in Beckenham, he sits semi-naked being smeared with make-up under the skylight of a one-storey building with a wooden gable roof squatting meekly amid a row of tall Victorian townhouses.

Across the street, chambermaids at the Swiss Cottage Holiday Inn are changing the sheets ready to be soiled by the arrival of the next touring rock band and their stage-door Jezebels, completely unaware that at this very moment, just over the road, the star at the top of this week's pops is shooting the cover of his new album.

Only a few days ago David received his first gold disc for sales of his last one. Every day now brings more fans outside his front door, ringing his bell, ripping souvenir plants out of his garden, causing his ageing landlord Mr Hoy no end of vandalised grief. Every week self-styled 'Bowie freaks' fill the letters pages and classifieds of the pop papers with words of unhinged lust and rages of holy war against all who dare besmirch his infinite fabulousness. His lookalikes stretch from the youth clubs of the South to the terraces of the North, with incoming tabloid reports of a new breed of football hooligan at Elland Road warpainting their faces with fright masks to ape *'tinselled pop idol David Bowie'*. He's the cover of *Melody Maker*, a poster in *Romeo*, a life-story comic strip in *Mirabelle* and an LP prop in an aspirational lifestyle advert for Access credit card in *TV Times*. His current single 'The Jean Genie' is fast outselling all competition at 20,000 copies a day, and even if the BBC stubbornly refuse to certify it above Satan's own pipsqueak Little Jimmy Osmond, as far as the *Maker*, the *New Musical Express* and the *Daily Mirror* are concerned, as of midnight on Sunday it, and he, will be number 1. Whether teen mag or tabloid, facts are facts in black-and-white. At 26 years old, David Bowie is a superstar.

Not just any old superstar. *'A super-terrestrial superstar,'* say the papers, taking their cue from the fans who send all those delirious *'Hero from the stars, all I ever ask is to touch you*' poems to *Record Mirror*. David is a superstar because Ziggy is a superstar, the character he invented as his living rock'n'roll camouflage for that gold album, *The Rise And Fall Of Ziggy Stardust And The Spiders From Mars*. The strange thing being, Ziggy, as David wrote him, never came from outer space. He only sang about it. But somewhere between the dyed red hair, the space-age clothes and the lyrics about a Starman in the sky the kids made up their own minds. Now nothing David can do or say could convince them otherwise. And why would he want to? In pebbledashed semis the felt tips are still scribbling verses of crazy cosmic love. '*We float across the moon, and pluck silver daisies from a sky of velvet, my Starman.*' If it's alien glamour they want, he's happy to take it all the way. Out beyond the stars, to the coldest reaches of the far-flung universe. Even to a funny little hut in Swiss Cottage.

Half a century ago it was the studio of a man who painted in light and colour making stained-glass windows. Now it belongs to a fashion photographer who's just made some of the world's most beautiful women look like sexless blobs of diecast plastic for this year's Pirelli calendar.

His name is Duffy, a short, balding, fussy man with a very short fuse whose task today is to make David look how a superstar ought to. Not flesh and bone but made of the same stuff the gods are made of. Stars. Moonbeams. Fire. Ice. Electricity. Thunder.

'Lightning.'

This is David's only instruction. He wants his new album sleeve to include some form of thunderbolt motif, perhaps somewhere on his body.

'Like a flash symbol.'

Duffy scratches his scruffy beard and shuffles off to the studio kitchen. Seconds later he's back with what looks like a casserole dish with a plug swinging from the bottom. It's his mum's old National rice cooker. Above the small control panel on the front sits the brand insignia: a circle punctured with two perfect little red and blue lightning bolts, top and bottom.

'Like that?' asks Duffy, pointing to the logo.

'Yes,' says David. 'Exactly that.'

Then a foreign voice.

'Heez face!'

It trills from the slim, lion-haired creature in the corner wearing a denim one-piece with an embroidered phoenix on the chest: his lips glossy with Eight Hour Cream, his skin glowing from regular moisturising with Beetham's Glycerine and Cucumber Milk, his smoky kohl eyes carefully scrutinising David's features as an artist might a blank canvas.

'Let me draw eet on heez face.'

Not two weeks since Britain joined the Common Market, everyone is doing their bit to celebrate the New Europe. *The Sun* do their bit by pondering '*What do French girls wear in bed?*' and enlightening their readers with the necessary pictorial evidence. The *Daily Mail* do their bit by slapping the Labour benches and other isolationist cynics with a rousing front-page ra-ra-ra: '*Ask yourselves how much hope and glory this land of ours would really enjoy if left on its own?*' The National Federation of Meat Traders do their bit by retorting we'll soon be '*a nation of macaroni eaters*'. Slade do their bit by selling out a 'Fanfare for Europe' concert at the London Palladium where their knicker-tossing fans bounce so violently they crack the balcony. And David Bowie is doing his bit by letting a Frenchman draw all over his face.

His name is Pierre Laroche and he's as French as his gorgeously Gallic name suggests with an extra string of onions and a beret on top. He used to work for Elizabeth Arden, now he's a freelance make-up artist who's already tickled his brush over the cheeks of Marc Bolan and his 'favoreet male face', Marc's stupidly good-looking T. Rex accomplice Mickey Finn. Like most people recruited into David's life with the sole purpose of improving his image, it was his wife Angie, not present today, who found and hired Pierre. And possibly it's the fact that she did and Duffy didn't which explains the strained Anglo-Franco relations as Pierre starts to apply his first rococo strokes to David's temple.

'No, no, not fucking like that!'

Duffy snatches a lipstick.

'A fucking big one!'

And scrawls the outline of an enormous zigzag down the centre of David's head.

'Now fill that in!'

Pierre plucks it back from Duffy's hand, batting his eyelids like twin guillotines. '*Alors.*'

Patiently, David sits still as five minutes become thirty become sixty, feeling the Frenchman's stick and brush softly stroking back and forth over his skin, massaging his brow, slanting down over his right eye, delicately over, under and around the lid, thinly back up to the bone of his shaved left eyebrow before crayoning sharply back down to the right side of his chin.

'*Et voilà!*'

Pierre steps aside so David can finally see in the dressing-table mirror. His face. His spectacular new face. Slashed red, black and blue from crown to jaw, like his head has been cleanly cleaved in two, splitting apart to expose raw blood and flesh beneath a metallic android shell. A face that once seen can never be unseen, branding itself on the eyeballs like its own graphic thunderbolt.

Ringflash primed and Hasselblad loaded, Duffy pokes his head beneath the camera hood and orders David into position.

'OK, now, head to the right.'

Click!

'Bit more.'

Click!

'All the way to the left.'

Click!

'Chin up. That's it.'

Click!

'Now facing me.'

Click!

'Look up.'

Click!

'Back to me.'

Click!

'Now straight ahead with your eyes closed.'

CLICK!

One frame. One image. One face. One that after today David will never wear again. He doesn't need to. History his rod, its lightning has struck.

DEATH AND REGENERATION. One identity vanishes and a new one assumes its place. It can happen in the stroke of a lipstick. The blink of a camera shutter. The splash of a coffin into its watery grave.

The coffin is black like the scantily clad pallbearers – six leggy models in leotards, stockings, top hats and elbow gloves – its lid and sides decorated with sequined shooting stars. It is made of cardboard but strong enough to bear the contents of one publicity photograph of the deceased and an accompanying single they recorded many years ago. Leading the funeral aboard a barge named the *Sloop John B* on a Sunday afternoon in the middle of the Thames is Radio 1 disc jockey Alan 'Fluff' Freeman. He wears a priest's smock and swings a thurible of burning incense. Beside him, the overdressed chief mourner reads aloud a eulogy from the lid's brass plaque.

'*Here lie the remains of dear Paul Raven,*
Although we tried so hard to save 'im,
Let's cast away this load of litter,
And raise a glass to Gary Glitter.'

In name as in sparkly jacket, the chunky 28-year-old who considers himself the third biggest pop act in Britain 'after Slade and T. Rex' grins for the few gathered members of the press. The arm that isn't in a sling after tripping backstage at a gig up north jovially slaps the coffin lid. Dear Paul Raven. The first miserable failed attempt by the boy born Paul Gadd to become a rock'n'roll star in a ready steady Sixties that refused to let him go. Now, reborn as Gary Glitter, with two Top 10 hits under his straining belt, a Kensington flat in the same block as *Nearest and Dearest*'s Jimmy Jewel and a chauffeur called Douglas to drive him around in a silver Jensen Interceptor, he believes he's living his destiny.

'There are a few people like Marc Bolan and Marilyn Monroe and me who have a certain magic.'

Today's vanishing trick with a cardboard coffin is his not-very-well-attended publicity stunt to notify the press of the release of a new single, 'Do You Wanna Touch Me?' A question presumably aimed at his many female followers, the youngest, according to his fan club secretary, being aged 4½. Gary says he even gets letters from 13-year-olds telling him they think of him '*as I make love to my boyfriend*'. Others prefer to share their disturbed passions in open letters to *Mirabelle*.

'*Dear Gary . . . I'm more afraid of you than I am in love . . . I see in you something that has been hurt and is bitter . . .*'

They're right, of course. That's what the burial of Paul Raven is for. Nailing shut all that pain, anger and bitterness, the childhood damage, the corrupting demons, the shameful secrets, the fuse of Mr Hyde's ticking time bomb, drowning the lot of it like a kitten in a sack. Rubbing out the wrong version of Paul Gadd like he never happened. No wounds, no scars, no nightmares. Nothing except the sequined façade of the right Paul Gadd. Gary Glitter, the court jester of glam. *Come along, kiddie-winkies! Do you wanna touch him?*

SPLOSH!

The coffin is ceremonially shoved overboard into a Thames the colour of diarrhoea. For a second it bobs awkwardly like a giant piece of flotsam. Then, with a sudden glug, it plunges below the surface, Gary watching it sink with lips that smile but eyes that scream. Down, down, out of sight, out of memory, down, down to the unseeable mud, sludge and slime of the city's river graveyard. Full fathom five, Paul Raven lies. Among the dead dreams, dead loves and dead hopes of a million dead yesterdays. Dead fathers' stopped stopwatches, dead mothers' till-death-parted wedding bands, dead toy soldiers and dolls' heads of dead sons and daughters, dead muggers' blades and dead stick-up mobs' pistols, dead tramps' tin cans and dead Sunday best china, dead war medals and dead rubber johnnies, dead bicycle frames and dead pram wheels, the sunken skulls of dumb suicides and dumber accidents, the murdered, the not missed, the never found and the couldn't swim, some rotting in the clay bed for years, decades, centuries while the uncaring metropolis above poured ever more dead shit upon their dead corpses and built bridge after bridge to block out the sun. And now the coffin of dead Paul Raven, black cardboard and papier-mâché slowly disintegrating in the current as the river flushes its endless armada of death out towards the North Sea, lapping at the banks to its own macabre rhythm, softly eavesdropping on the alien sounds of the living city. The wolf whistles and smokers' coughs of the not yet dead, vendors yelling 'Staaan-dud!', shouts of 'nice one, Cyril!' and beeping black cabs. And here by the South Bank, as tiny spicks and specks of Paul Raven's decaying soul are dragged along on the dead tide of Old Father Thames, the echo of one man and his guitar singing a song about death. His death.

'*My death . . .*'

David Bowie, looking ghostly pale but as kissably alive as any man wearing strap platforms decorated with palm tree heels can be, is in

Studio 3 of London Weekend Television singing a gloomy Jacques Brel number. He wears the same silvery blue lurex jacket he wore two weeks ago on *Top of the Pops*, though this being only a rehearsal, by the time the cameras roll he'll have changed into another the public haven't seen: a geometric blue-and-red mosaic pattern with giant crimson notch lapels that make his rust red hair seem even rustier, offset with a lurex polka-dot shirt and tie and a lone diamante chandelier dangling from his right ear. Every stitch, save earring, shoes and understockings, exclusively designed for him by his close friend and personal tailor Freddie, or 'Fred of the East End' as he now markets himself: you can't buy his clothes off the peg and he doesn't make them for anyone else. Freddie's here in the dressing room, pursing lips, pinching collars and ruffling sleeves alongside Suzi, David's empress of Elnett hairspray, and the now already indispensable Pierre, hands flapping back and forth across David's face like a weaver on a loom as he brushes a waxy alabaster white foundation, the faintest sfumato of Bourjois rouge on the cheeks, pink frosted cream around his eyes and a glossy smear of Elizabeth Arden balm on his lips. The finished effect is beautiful. Dead beautiful. Like a handsome corpse prettified by a master undertaker, newly risen from his open coffin in clothes even a pharaoh would protest were too grand to be buried in.

All this obsessive preparation is to bewitch the viewers of a new chat show hosted by an unmarried 38-year-old former English teacher from Lancashire named Russell Harty. He's LWT's latest weapon in the weekend ratings war against the BBC's established rival from the other side of the Pennines, Michael Parkinson, with both programmes jousting head-to-head at 11 p.m. on a Saturday night. According to the *Evening Standard*, Russell is just edging the lead, despite possessing a technique they liken to '*sheer amateurism*' and a manner that dares them to question if he's entirely heterosexual.

'Yes, well – I don't know,' blushes Russell. 'How do we know? We don't know who's going to walk around the corner.'

Walking around today's corner on palm tree heels, David is pre-recording a spot that won't air until the middle of February when he'll be edited into that week's *Russell Harty Plus* between a member of the cast of *Upstairs, Downstairs* and a champion showjumper. Those who wouldn't rather watch Parky flirting unsuccessfully with Maggie Smith on BBC One will see him sing two songs between 12 minutes grinding his teeth at the mercy of Russell's fruity interrogation: about his shoes, his stockings, his earring, his home, his faith, his philosophy, his fan mail, his bisexuality and his thoughts on groupies, male and female, each question delivered with a stemware-twiddling purr as if he's forgotten to add 'duckie' at the end of the sentence.

'You have a strange face (duckie).'

'Yes,' says David. 'It's a mask.'

'You wouldn't like to take it off (duckie)?'

'I couldn't. I've lived with it so long I think it's just raw blood and flesh underneath now.'

'You make it sound very painful (duckie)?'

'Yes.'

And so it stumbles on like a bad exercise in police entrapment, Russell saucily pitching, David defensively putting, the audience giggling in nervous fits until the cue to return to the stage area, take his stool, strap on his guitar and sing a sad Belgian chanson about unavoidable death. Levity leaves the building with the first sombre chord. In the spotlight David suddenly looks more undead than dead – a troubadour Nosferatu only a sunset away from puncturing another virgin's jugular. His voice seizes the audience just as savagely. A raw blood and flesh voice from the man underneath the mask. His guitar, the coffin. Brel's words, the nails. His eyes, the sequined stars. But whose death he's foreseeing is anyone's guess. The boy who once was David Jones? The pop star David Bowie? The rock'n'roll monster Ziggy Stardust?

Beyond the studio walls, the lifeless river keeps on flowing.

TWO

YOU CAN'T QUITE SEE THE THAMES from the ninth-floor penthouse of the Inn on the Park. Just Hyde Park to the west, Buckingham Palace to the south and the Post Office Tower poking proudly in the north. Or you would if the windows weren't sealed to deny even the teeniest sliver of daylight.

It's been like this up here since Christmas when the whole floor was modified to the demands of one filthy rich guest who's yet to set foot outside on London's streets, spending every day in this room.

That's him, lying on a loose patchwork of paper towels, there as a shield between whatever germs lurk in the freshly laundered bedding beneath, stark naked. He usually is, apart from when he has meetings with one of his entourage when he throws on a bathrobe or a pair of drawstring shorts. A painfully thin old man, weighing not much over eight stone, his face gaunt and unshaven, his scratched skin like tissue paper, the uncut nails on his fingers and toes twisted like thorns. If it wasn't for that slight regular bobbing motion in his chest, you might think he'd been dredged straight from the bottom of the dead river.

His last meal comprised of two custard desserts. Perhaps in another 12 hours he'll eat another one. The only other solids to have slipped in his mouth today are his blue Valium tablets. Sometimes he forgets to keep count and swallows up to 40 times his recommended daily dose. In between he likes to inject himself regularly with codeine. Sometimes the needles break off in his skin: many are still embedded there. Now and again an aide will check in on him and report to their fellow staff: 'He looked like he was in the outer spaces.' But never at any point does he forget who he is. And if he ever did, the newspapers he has sent up to his room every day are always there to remind him.

'*Howard Hughes the American millionaire recluse who refuses to see the Press – or anyone else, for that matter – has an original way of finding out about any country he visits. He sends out members of his staff equipped with movie cameras to record the sights, and possible investments, of the place. Then, in the silence of his lonely hotel room, he plays back these extraordinary home movies.*'

This is true. He has a projector set up here at all times. When not on the phone, often talking to someone sat in the next room for fear they may bring in more germs, or eating custard-based desserts, or miscounting his pills, or stabbing himself with opiates, he spends a lot of his day, every day, watching movies. Sometimes the same one over and over again. Some he's seen a hundred times or more.

The projector is running right now, wobbling its picture on the screen opposite. Something old and black-and-white with Marlene Dietrich. And there watching her on his raft of paper towels lies the world-famous American millionaire recluse Howard Hughes. Most definitely naked. Obviously doped. Probably insane.

Nine floors below him, London is at full-throttle sinful Saturday night. If he had the strength, Mr Hughes could throw on a bathrobe and slippers and see it for himself. Not five minutes round the corner, the brasses in Shepherd's Market are standing waiting to solicit him. Stagger on a bit further and he'd reach Piccadilly Circus where the red light of Coca-Cola shines in the dull glassy eyes of teen runaways turned hustlers hanging on the railings they call 'the Meat Rack' by the steps down to the Tube. If he was still feeling brave, he could cross over under the giant Wrigley's sign into a sprocket-holed Soho of the sort of films his projector never sees. *I Am Available*, *Unsatisfied Virgins*, *Seven Times a Day*, *Dagmar's Hot Pants*, *Sex Nest* and *Bedroom Mazurka*. On he might stumble, by now starting to sicken with the pimp-greasing smell of men doing whatever they believe they must in order to feel like the men they think they should be. Potsloshing jeerers and down-in-oners, bra-clasp-fumblers and one-minute-pumpers, in-the-mouthers and likes-em-youngers, carpet dribblers and brewer's droopers. Tottering hellward, through desperate hippies trying to score Chinese junk cut with strychnine, dodging strip club mumblers and doorway barterers. '*It's three quid, love. For six it gets better, for ten it's really nice, and for fifty I'm wicked.*' Until he'd finally blunder into a crooked alleyway just off Dean Street, coming to rest in the shadows, leaning against a wall to catch his breath.

And just supposing that he did, instead of still lying zonked before a movie screen in his ninth-floor hotel suite, then Mr Hughes would be just inches of brick away from a man in a brown velvet cap, chequered shirt and loose trousers, drawing hard on a Marlboro, sitting in the control room of Trident Studios watching his smoke waltz to a sad and strange melody.

'Aladdin Sane (1913–1938–197?)'

The title track of the new album David's rushing to finish in the next four days before he sails back to America. Most of its songs were written over there on his last visit. A collection of heavy fucked-up postcards from a heavy fucked-up continent. Looming dystopia between Seattle and Phoenix. Sleaze in Los Angeles. Squalor in New York. Panic in Detroit. Death in New Orleans.

And battle cries over the Atlantic, where the words for 'Aladdin Sane' were drafted last December, homeward bound aboard the RHMS *Ellinis* with his wife Angie, soon to be reunited with their baby son Zowie. Before they docked in Southampton she told him she was pregnant again. This time, no corks were popped. Their sleeping patterns of the past three months made easy arithmetic. David knew it probably wasn't his, just as Angie knew that somewhere in the country they'd left behind his cells were probably multiplying in wombs that weren't hers. She spent the rest of the voyage sick in their cabin bed as he sat reading *Vile Bodies*, dwelling on dead roses and sad remains. They got home just in time for Christmas when David played a concert for the children's charity Dr Barnardo's.

Angie had an abortion.

'*Ba, ba, ba, ba, ba-ba.*'

The stillbirth of 'Aladdin Sane'. A Guernica grey song of war, decadence and despair sounding like three records playing at the same time: a Cole Porter shellac 78 wobbling on a wind-up gramophone; a

Béla Bartók piano sonata jump-scratching wildly on a stereo radiogram; and a funky single by David Bowie and The Spiders From Mars fuzzing from a coffee bar jukebox. All haunting the same time and space like the combined noise of the twentieth century crumpling in on itself in singular counterpoint – the jazz age, post-tonal classical modernism and glam rock imploding as one sonic black hole sucking the listener towards an unheard future. A sound no normal human being in their right mind ought ever have conceived.

He doesn't sing it so much as haunt it, evaporating in and out of the ivory shellshock of his pianist, Mike Garson, whose showpiece solo is a self-contained loony tune sounding like Tom chasing Jerry up and down all 88 keys of a concert grand for a full minute and a half. It is audacious, unsettling and, commercially speaking, wholly unfit for airplay. It is also the best thing David has ever recorded.

So is the album: the best David has yet made. Something he's decided to call *Aladdin Sane*. A neurosis wrapped up in a pun that might be a whole new aspect of David Bowie or just a different version of Ziggy Stardust – a Ziggy who got what he wished for, now fatally wounded by the consequences. That's the difference, right there. The David who wrote *Ziggy Stardust* was still only imagining what it was like to be a famous rock'n'roll star: *Aladdin Sane* was written by a David who *knows* what it's like to be a famous rock'n'roll star. Ziggy was the idealised fantasy. Aladdin is the corrupted reality. The sound of vain purpose and moral emptiness, private hell and paradise lost, vile bodies and flushed foetuses.

A sound sad as the city beyond the bricks. Where a teenage redhead unzips for her next customer in a flat above the Blue Moon Club. Where tomorrow night the Palladium will see Gary Glitter ask a packed house of screaming prepubescents if they want to touch him. Where the baby-faced Dilly boys are still huddling along the Meat Rack selling innocence for a fiver. Too tired and too ruined to even begin to wonder what it would cost them to buy it back.

TEN DOLLARS. FOR that you'll get a soft-faced Puerto Rican boy just off the Greyhound to suck your cock in the nearest fleapit running *Deep*

Inside Melissa. That's about a buck a minute's worth, not including movie tickets and a couple of sodas. But if it's quality chicken you're after, you're gonna have to speak to the man. Ace the Spade or Hollywood Al on Times Square, or Mike Muscles over on 53rd and 3rd, or Super Sam or Cigar Murray down the Village. It'll cost you a good half-yard, twice that if you're the kind of chickenhawk who wants home delivery. But, boy, they'll box them up and drive them out any way you likes 'em, puppy-fat juicy and finger lickin' good, so doped up or so beat up from belts and cigarette burns that after the seventeenth rape chained to a bed they don't even know what 'no' *is* anymore. Demand is high and supply is endless. Every day the Port Authority bus terminal spits them out like a gumball machine, dumbass knapsack runaways from the industrial Midwest scared they might get whupped by their old man when he reads their flunked report card and truly believing nothing could be worse. Until they wind up 14-year-old catamites dancing the pervert chorus of 42nd Street.

Two years ago, two *long* years ago when things weren't quite so bad – before the pimps and junkies frightened everyone away from theatreland, before you couldn't find a single monument that wasn't vandalised with spray cans, before everyone in apartment blocks had learned never to use the elevator because there's less chance of being mugged on the stairs, before daytime stick-ups at the lights in Central Park were a certainty for any driver stupid enough to leave a window down, before parents had to teach their kids how to hand their money over to a stranger with a knife the way they used to teach them ABCs, before over 80 per cent of yellow cabs had bulletproof plexiglass fitted between the driver and the backseat, before armed guards in every major department store, before stories of being robbed and raped in your own home became commonplace as parking tickets, before old ladies sick of so many handbag snatches started carrying their money in plain brown grocery bags, before the exodus of the terrorised white middle class leaving the city to escape 'those animal blacks' began in earnest, before the ethnic melting pot became a raging furnace, before the Knapp Commission hearings when some folk still called the pigs 'the police', before the annual murder rate for a city of eight million reached ten times that of the entire British Isles – before any of that, this was the sidewalk-level New York City David met nose-to-nose on his first visit as a limey Joe Schmoe who didn't know his Downtown from his Up.

Two years later, an aerophobic English rock star arriving after a week at sea in a deluxe suite aboard the SS *Canberra*, he sees it all through limo glass. Watching the streets like bad television, he can switch over any time he likes, changing channels with every blink at a passing marquee. *Blink.* Peep Show. *Blink.* Rubs Showers Saunas. *Blink.* Coca-Cola. *Blink.* Jesus Saves. *Blink.* Adult Movies XXX. *Blink.* But some signs never change.

steak chick
lobster peas

However hot New York burns, Max's Kansas City fiddles on. David's hotel is only a few blocks round the corner in Gramercy Park, a leafy square between the sliding tankards of Pete's Tavern on 18th and *The Poseidon Adventure* playing on 23rd. He could walk it in five. He could also get stabbed in four. The limo takes a red-light six.

In his new multicoloured Freddie suit and orange scarf, he steps out of the car like a walking gypsy blanket. Stepping after him is Geoff, his old school friend from Bromley, whose curly hair and swarthy features are easily mistaken for 10cc's Graham Gouldman, and who David's just rescued from a job on a building trade magazine to join him on tour as his backing singer, sailing companion and general Tweedledum. Being with Geoff helps David to remember who he is. Or at least who he was.

Any other night at Max's and he'd head straight to the back room to be received like a visiting head of state by the plastic kings and nylon queens of Gotham's rock'n'roll nobility. But tonight David leads Geoff up the stairs, taking a front table near a small low stage backed by a red curtain, hoping that the man about to sit at the waiting electric organ is as great as he used to bore everyone about.

Biff Rose. David had clean forgotten about him, lately neither on his mind nor his turntable. Not until he docked in New York and saw an ad for his six nights at Max's, and like the taste of a tea-soaked madeleine he was suddenly 23 again, perched on a stool in the back of the Three Tuns in Beckenham, hair permed, eyebrows unshaved, a stripey jumper and an acoustic guitar, spreading the gospel of Saint Biff to a small spatter of hippie applause. The same thankless missionary instinct that blighted his *Hunky Dory* album with a cover of Biff's 'Fill Your Heart'. And even if he can no longer remember *why* exactly he recorded it, he can still remember the devout urge of *wanting* to. Which is why he's sitting upstairs at Max's with Geoff tonight.

When Biff shuffles on he's as mailman ordinary as David expected from the sleeves of his worn albums back home: a sad cake of a face iced with a black moustache and a boy scout's smile. Not a rock'n'roll face, but then Biff isn't a rock'n'roll act: he's musical funny papers. The only problem being he's a far better pianist than he is a comedian, as proven by the next hour spent whining ironic one-liners about hamburgers, garbage and Jesus in a comb-and-paper-thin voice over whimsical vaudeville keyboard. The half-full Max's crowd laugh chewing-gum-laughs, but no bellies boom and no sides are split, not even David's, though he claps the loudest and grins the hardest. The strained grin of having just realised you can no more feed a dead memory than you can a dead cat.

Poor old Biff. It's not been his week. He started his residency here last Wednesday as the headliner, but after the first few evenings he's been leapfrogged by the popularity of his support act to become second on his own bill. Not that David realises until after Biff bumbles off and nobody at the surrounding tables leaves. If anything, it feels like only now the room's starting to fill.

Before he has a chance to ask why, a short figure scuffs on stage with an acoustic guitar, wearing jeans and an open shirt exposing a smooth hairless chest. He has a farmhand's tan, a leading man's chin, sleepy eyes and a dark scraggly beard: if you threw a tea towel over his head, he'd look just like a disciple from *King of Kings*. He gazes out with a smile of relaxed confidence, maybe too relaxed, testing his tuning with gentle plucks, saying 'gud evenin'' in such a lazy cowpoke's croak everyone, including David, immediately assumes he's stoned. But, at the age of 22, he's never had a toke in his life.

He begins with a slow strummed misery, rhyming '*deceivin*'' with '*believin*'' and '*noose*' with '*loose*', which couldn't be more Dylanish if he sang it in shades and a curly wig. Not so very long ago, David was guilty of the same cheap imitation, and for that reason alone he takes an instant dislike. The second song is just as glum. David and Geoff are four swigs and a stubbed cigarette away from slinking off when the scraggly little man suddenly swaps acoustic for a wooden Telecaster. 'Ker mon out,' he shouts, and the stage swamps with a road gang of slept-in T-shirts and jeans along with a tall black man wielding a saxophone. Its brass gleam immediately catches David's eye. Amps buzz and a bass drum thuds. 'OK,' smiles scraggly. 'One. Two. One, two, three, four . . .'

The sound strips the skin from David's teeth. A taut swinging energy that oughtn't to come from such sweaty raggle tagglers, freewheeling and moondancing, neither rock nor soul but tough and funky as both. The scraggly words still bop like Dylan, but the right supercharged Dylan: a blonder on blonde bringing even more back home Dylan jiving about Bronx ballerinas and Ferris wheels. Words that singe the hairs on the back of David's neck, as it hits him hard as being mowed down by a bus on 82nd Street that he may no longer be the best songwriter in the room.

But he can't help swallow his pride and clap his palms raw for the little bastard. The *brilliant* little bastard. As the advertising department of Columbia Records put it, '*This man puts more thoughts, more ideas and images into one song than most people put into an album.*' Scraggly's debut LP came out only a few weeks ago, and though not many people have bought it yet, tomorrow David will increase its sales by a significant one, playing it repeatedly in his sixth-floor hotel room, studying every groove and printed lyric with the jealous zeal of a master forger, more unsure than ever whether America can love a man pretending he's Aladdin Sane.

Not now it's been kissed by Bruce Springsteen.

THREE

VALENTINE'S DAY, and the skies above New York can't help but weep with laughter. It soaks the skulking bums only a few mugged bucks from their veins' next date with Cupid's arrow, splashing off the windscreens of the yellow cabs skimming up Sixth Avenue to where hours of pancaking, liplining, eyeshadowing, lashcurling, glittersticking, blushering and blowdrying wilt damply under the neon marquee of Radio City Music Hall. The crazy keen have been queuing here in the cold and wet since lunchtime for a show that doesn't start until eleven. But if you're Salvador Dalí, you wait till gone half ten then take a limo the five short blocks from your hotel straight to the kerb by the guests' entrance without one raindrop skooshing the points of your moustache.

It tugs the rest of his face like reins toward the golden foyer, where a giant mural depicting the futile dream of the Fountain of Youth looms over the stairwell, unnoticed by those most in need of remembering it. The sight of Dalí's waxed antennae immediately reassures them theirs must indeed be the hottest tickets in town. Six thousand of them, waiting for the rip of an usher directing the Bloomingdaled famous and the homesewn freaky to their velvet seats down in the stalls or up in the three mezzanine balconies.

Front of house, naturally, sit the VIPs – no P being more I than the conspicuous blonde bouncing a zeppelin-shaped inflated condom on her knee, waiting for her husband to make his grand entrance.

Her husband. That's the top and bottom, gals. Anything and anyone between is just another piece of ass burning his hotel mattress until the next knock on the door. Like the one she found him with only this week, some black waitress who damned near turned white when she opened the door and saw her standing there in a fur coat with a smile like the grille of a Cadillac running her over. She let David introduce her. 'Angela, my wife.' You heard him. His *wife*. She who must be obeyed, OK, sister? So here's the deal. On the road he fucks who he must when she's elsewhere fucking who she must – having learned the hard way on the last tour never to do so under each other's noses – but once her mules click–clack back in town the show's over, sweetie. Because any minute now he's going to be grinding that stage floor and this whole place will pop with screams. Screaming at his clothes, his hair, his make-up, at everything that made kids bus in from out of state to stand in the rain like lost trick-or-treaters in jerry-built drag, some armed with Valentine's cards to toss from the balconies bleeding 'Oh you pretty thing, we love you madly!' in purple felt tip. Well, just *who* do you think got the pretty thing his clothes, his hair, his make-up in the first place? The quilted stitches of Freddie Burretti, the chop and colour of Suzi Fussey, the cream and powder of Pierre Laroche?

'ANGIE!'

Don't ever forget it. She brought every one of them into his life, same as she brought the gleeful Japanese man in the shaggy coat sitting here tonight, three seats along on the other side of Pierre. It was Angie who found David his first piece of Kansai Yamamoto clothing last year. Now Kansai's here, not long off a flight from Tokyo, having cabbed straight from the airport to witness more of his expensive and elaborate creations wrapped around her husband's '*super-terrestrial*' body. Pick any thread of David's and you'll usually find Angie holding the original spool. And he knows it, just like in the song he wrote for her, the one he'll be singing later. '*You and I . . .*' You, Angie: I, David. Hear that, bitches?

So there go the lights, and here come those screams, and up flies her arm, and away floats the condom, and bright as a bomb-blast flash Angie's teeth. A smile that only comes with knowing you're indispensable.

The very same thought accompanied by a cooler facial expression illuminates the hippocampus of another brain not so very far away: one swathed by a curly scalp, perfumed by Havana smoke and sentried by toady eyes that seldom blink for fear of missing anything that might further the world domination enterprise of Tony Defries. The satisfaction that even if it's not his name on tonight's ticket, as David's manager it will be on the takings. Because whatever colour the clothes, the hair or the paint on the face of the thing that hits that stage tonight, it's merely a product. *His* product. Like it says on the *Space Oddity* LP nudging inside this week's American Top 50. 'David Bowie is a Mainman artist.' Yes, and Tony Defries is the Mainman mainman. Which makes David Bowie the box of cornflakes and Tony Defries the Mr Kellogg.

See, all of this Radio City razzmatazz shouldn't really be happening, not to someone who's sold as comparatively few records in America as David has. But it is, exactly as Defries promised it would from the outset of their last US tour, a no-limo-spared champagne showboat staged to convince the press of a success David hadn't yet achieved. Mainman couldn't possibly afford it. Nor could David's record company, RCA, though Defries made sure they got stuffed with the bill. And why this tour they've stuffed him straight back by refusing to pay expenses beyond necessary hotels and travel.

But, at this point, who cares? What matters is the jean genie's now out of the bottle. The superstar fiction made sufficient American newsprint to become superstar fact. Enough here in New York that a singer who five months ago couldn't quite fill Carnegie Hall now packs out two nights in a venue twice the size. All that nickels-and-dimes business of selling records he can leave to RCA. Defries is in the stocks-and-shares business of selling the brand. BOWIE™. Of course, they might argue that without David there'd be nothing for him to sell. But Defries being Defries, casting his eyes up and around tonight's 6,000 customers, he doesn't see it that way. Without him, there'd *be* no David to buy.

So there go the lights, and here come the screams, and soft sucks his cigar, and out puffs the smoke, and firm as a clam clench Defries's teeth. In a smile that only comes with knowing you're indispensable.

Similar opinions fostering stonier Yorkshire grimaces linger in the wings as the darkness descends. The feeling of vengeful gods with the power to tear down paradise should they dare. *One out, all out!* All it would take is to turn round and march straight out the stage door before the entrance music from *A Clockwork Orange* ends. Then David would appear, blinking in horror like a general leading his last lame troops towards certain death the moment he realised all he had left was his pianist, Garson, and the four new back-up musicians hired for this tour: two saxophonists, his friend Geoff with a pair of congas and his old pal Hutch on rhythm guitar. Because what bite has David Bowie without the amplified venom of his three Spiders From Mars? None, and his rhythm section of Trevor Bolder and Woody Woodmansey know it. Same as they know their guitarist and Hull shipmate Mick Ronson is on more money than they are. That's understandable: he's been playing with him longer, and in terms of fundamentals is only marginally less vital to David's music than mains electricity. They just didn't know that they're still being paid less than Garson, the new boy of five months. Until he accidentally told them, the catalyst for yesterday's ugly showdown in David's hotel suite. David sat quiet and emotionless. Defries listened with eyes of cold anger. Mick and Trevor traded grumbles about fair wages, thinking it best to let Woody's hothead steam their grievances for them. Soon wishing they hadn't. Because whatever Woody's learned from the strange literature Garson's been feeding him lately about '*the road to total freedom*', he evidently still has a lot of work to do '*auditing*' his '*engrams*'. Otherwise he might not have called David 'a cunt'.

So there go the lights, and here come the screams, and Woody rubs his drumsticks, and Trevor takes the weight of his bass, and Mick checks the pickup volume on his Les Paul. But though each believes they're indispensable, not one of them is smiling.

Far up above them, higher than Defries's wafting smoke, higher than Angie's drifting condom, hidden by the proscenium and unseen by everyone except his black Yorkshire bodyguard, Stuey, and a couple of stagehands, David dangles in near darkness. He's wearing a black and silver vinyl bodysuit, flared out in giant semicircles on each leg making him look like one of Dalí's melting clocks. In the centre of his forehead is a gold circle, put there by Pierre using a new German make-up cake he found here in New York, a bit like a third eye. All that stands between him and the ground is a small circular platform at the centre of a silver gyroscope, large enough for a man of his size to stand in the middle gripping the central thread, and 60 feet of thin air. One false move and – SPLAT! Angie becomes a widow, BOWIE™ becomes BOWIE R.I.P.

and The Spiders From Mars can stop fretting about being ripped off and find another singer. That's why David doesn't look down, only straight ahead, listening to the blood pulsing in his ears above the batlike screams and the gathering crescendo of the *Clockwork Orange* overture rattling the speakers. Suddenly a winch turns and the platform starts to drop. A bead of sweat trickling down his back, heart thumping, he's aware only of descending motion and the strobes flickering madly below like an approaching runway. Down, down goes David. To the light and the noise. To the eyes of Dalí and the ears of deaf adoration. To the mutineers, hucksters and hellcats. Like a coffin plunging overboard.

Down, down goes David.

ALL THE WAY DOWN. Not until the very end of the concert, after 21 songs, four costume changes and an intermission where noses are powdered to a tape of David's current favourites, including Frank Sinatra's 'My Funny Valentine', Lou Reed's 'Walk On The Wild Side' and The Royal Teens' 'Short Shorts'. But down he goes, slap on the final ta-dah of 'Rock 'N' Roll Suicide' just as a male fan vaults the stage and pelts towards him for an embrace. Hitting the deck, out cold, the crowd gasping unsure if this is merely part of his act, scooped up by security and carted off like a body from a battlefield to a panicking dressing room where it takes many minutes of frantic brow-mopping and no shortage of volunteers for mouth-to-mouth before he comes round. The official explanation given to the press is 'a lack of eating and sleeping'.

Back in Room 602 of the Gramercy Park Hotel, he conks out for twelve hours solid.

As David sleeps, an ocean away England awakes. To the shake of milk crates, the sizzle of fat and the transistor squeak of Tony Blackburn. The number 1 sound of Common Market Britain is 'Blockbuster', a castrato cousin of 'The Jean Genie' as conceived by the 'ChinniChap' writer-producer team of Nicky Chinn and Mike Chapman and played to order by The Sweet, a band with all the glamour of a Peterborough picket line until they became the kind of Ziggy-come-latelys *19* magazine denounces as '*the aspirant Bowies who have simply succeeded in making an individual's personal expression of sexuality look like just another cheap sham*'.

As justification, guitarist Andy Scott proudly points such critics to their four gold discs and snaps, 'We did the right thing in adopting the poof image.'

Fourteen places and a country road behind them, Olivia Newton-John isn't convinced. 'I just don't like the glitter,' she argues Aussiely on behalf of all Sheilas who want their Bruces to be Bruces. 'I like men to be men and not tarted up. I find men in make-up distasteful.'

An opinion shared by her good friend, the Reverend Cliff Richard.

'I really dig David Bowie's music,' says Cliff. 'But his campness kills it for me. Bowie is physically a man, no matter what he does, and I think it must be pretty confusing for his audiences. I mean, it doesn't help young people when they see him like *that*.'

They see him, they see her, they see him. Or is it her?

'Every day I'm a creature of a different mood and this is just one of them.'

Six foot one in her stockings, '*with glorious Eiffel Towers where other women have legs*' as the *Express* puts it, the blonde blue-eyed German countess born Vera but known as 'Veruschka' is certainly the tallest, allegedly the most expensive and probably the most beautiful model in the world. She also makes a striking bloke in her latest advert for Tonik mohair suits for men.

'*A fusion of beauty and sophistication. An aristocratic equation of arrogance and style. An infinitude of experience with a slight touch of evil.*'

And a better-looking geezer than David Bowie.

Or maybe not, seeing him now sleeping serenely in his New York hotel bed, Angie watching over him, as she always watches over him. Man and wife. Just not your typical heterosexual man and wife. Not even bisexual.

'Transexual,' decides Angie.

Yes. That's a better word to sum up her and David. A right saucy pair of Veruschkas.

'The word bisexual suggests limits, that we have as many sexual taboos as more repressed people. We believe that human beings are all capable of sexual feeling and that they let it out in any direction they most naturally want to. A lot of parents have screwed their kids up really bad by saying being queer is dirty and you'll never get a good job if you're a lesbian.

That shouldn't be true. A lot of the kids need liberating from all that nonsense.'

Angie's thoughts race on. 'You know what I'd like to see?' She smiles to herself. 'I'd like LIVE SEX shows before every performance so the kids could see for themselves what's going on! What's available to them!'

Three thousand miles across the sea, Cliff Richard is praying hard.

FOUR

HE LOOKS LIKE HE COULD BE DEAD. He often does, floating in the pool not moving a muscle, mouth open, eyes closed like a shipwrecked corpse. Every now and then his friend Leee has to jump in and haul him out, just to make sure he's still alive, which he always is. More or less. It's just that he's not actually *living*. He's existing. A creature that spends every day here in paradise, tanning, floating, drinking, fucking and pumping enough junk in his veins to forget how much he hates his life. Except it isn't. *His* life? Not anymore. And that's the tourniquet-tugging problem.

'Iggy?'

He squints enough of an eye open to see a silhouette by the poolside.

'You OK?'

'Yeah,' he tells Leee with a groggy moan. And throws another crackling lie on the bonfire.

Iggy is not OK. He hasn't been in weeks. Not since he and his Stooges moved into this shady oasis hairpinned way up in the Hollywood Hills among sagebrush, fan palms and the randy ghost of Errol Flynn.

It was all Defries's idea. Stick Iggy and the band in the Californian sun with Leee taking care of everything as Mainman's babysitter. Keep them busy and out of trouble by finding them a rehearsal space a short drive down the hill on Santa Monica Boulevard where they can hone their amplified ruckus while they wait to be given further instructions. And wait. And wait.

And wait.

And drink. And fix. And float. And try not to think. That's what the Courvoisier and heroin's for. Because if Iggy starts to think, he'll cease to float and start to sink, down into the bitter black depths where the bad thoughts swim. The paranoid piranhas that want to tell him what a dumb fuck he is for still believing Tony Defries is his saviour.

Saviour?

Oh, Iggy. Wake up! So he took you on and got you a record deal when you were on your hunkers, but only because his golden boy David made him. But ask yourself – what, *really*, has he done for you since?

You fulfilled your half of the bargain. You made an album that's been ready since David finished mixing it four months ago, now finally being released in a sleeve you don't like because Defries didn't bother to consult you – which tells you everything you need to know about how little he values *Raw Power*. But the point is, right now, you really ought to be talking yourself hoarse to every journalist between here and Fleet Street about how it's going to save the future of rock'n'roll. Except you can't. Defries is still hung up on the same 'no access' bullshit he pulled for David. It's why in England the papers now call him 'Tony Deep Freeze'. So there aren't any interviews, just like there aren't any gigs either. He won't let you talk and he won't let you play. Not even locally down at the Whisky or any of the clubs on the Strip. He says they're too small and you're too big. But if that's the case, why won't he let you *play* big? Why doesn't he fix it for The Stooges to launch *Raw Power* with a tour around the UK? Jesus! *Imagine* the scenes! 'Search And Destroy' in Sheffield! 'Penetration' in Perth! 'Your Pretty Face Is Going To Hell' in Hull! It'd be like the birth of a new youth movement of topless little Iggys rampaging through the provinces in Dionysian ecstasy. Only it's never going to happen, is it? Look at your diary. An inkless blank, even though Leee's under orders to make sure you and your band of half-smacked fuckups still drag yourselves down to rehearsals. But for what?

Nothing. That's the sum total of what Tony Defries has done for you, Iggy. A big fat zero. Because you don't seriously think all *this* is something? A $900-a-week house in the Hills, blue skies, pink flowers, a

Cadillac in the garage and a school-age chick on a sun lounger waiting to blow you the moment you're out of that pool?

Nah, Ig. *This* ain't paradise. This is prison. Defries has locked you here and thrown away the key.

So, go ahead, cook up and bite down. You really might as well keep shooting that shit into your body. Because if Iggy Pop's not allowed to be Iggy Pop anymore, then, yes, he'd be better off dead.

'You OK, Iggy?'

Leee again.

'Uh-huh.'

The lie again.

Twisting around, Iggy softly splashes to the pool's edge and hauls himself out. He shakes the droplets from his bleached hair, grabs a towel and starts rubbing his taut toffee-brown body. The girl on the lounger sits up, pulling at the straps of her bikini top before following his wet footprints on the patio stones into the house.

Neither hear the passing convertible on Mulholland Drive, its roof down, its radio humming '*killing me softly*' as the drunken sun lazily blazes above.

WHEN IT EVENTUALLY SETS, fizzing into the Pacific like blacksmith's steel in a quenching bucket, the Angels of the City come out to play.

The ones who haven't already spent the day playing poolside hooky with idle junkies up Torreyson Drive have been smacking gum between classes in respectable junior highs. Their parents are rich enough to buy them anything they need and dumb enough to actually oblige. They want for nothing and try for less. That's the big difference between them and those poor chickens on the deuce in New York, on their knees in station johns because it's either suck or starve. No, these girls – and they are *girls* in all their menstrual infancy and clownish make-up – do it for fun. They have no need for pimps, only their egos, their only payment the priceless boast of allowing their 14-year-old bones to be jumped by an Englishman twice their age of sufficient repute in the racks of Tower Records. Other than that, the boys of Times Square and the girls of Sunset Strip are exactly the same. Chicken is chicken whichever way you fry it.

Their names are like makes of sports car. Sable, Lori, Sparky, Queenie and Shray. They have their own dress code, typically hot pants stretched tight over thin flat bottoms, halter necks strapped over skinny titless torsos, beads, floppy hats and star-shaped sunglasses, wobbling on wedge heels with painted toenails. They speak their own language about 'foxy ladies' 'making the scene' with 'far-out super dudes'. They even have their own magazine launched last month called *Star*, as in fucker. It's not so different from the British girls' mags, except where *Mirabelle* asks '*Could you marry a pop star?*' and *Jackie* asks '*If you had Donny Osmond for tea, what would you cook for him?*', *Star* asks '*Should you be satisfied with just one guy?*' between advice on nose jobs and make-up tips from the child-faced groupies to whom it grants endless celebrity. *Star* is printed proof that Western civilisation is accelerating to hell in something much faster than a handcart. But for those who need convincing in person there's always Rodney Bingenheimer's English Disco.

From the outside it looks nothing like the English disco it tries to be and everything like the Los Angeles sex parlour it pretends it isn't: a marquee with the owner's name surrounded by a chain of lights broken here and there by the odd blown bulb and a yellow sign with 'ENGLISH DISCO' in a pantomime approximation of Shakespearean script slapped on some wooden slats covering what would be a window.

Step inside, and you enter a bare-bricked dungeon where Anglophilia and paedophilia justify one another as conscience, or lack of, demands. Master of the dungeon is Rodney, the benign face of lecherous supply and demand blinking behind the tinted shades of a satin Rumpelstiltskin deluded he's identical twins with Ronnie Wood. His walls are splattered with assorted posters and record sleeves of English rock groups, most past or forthcoming attractions to the prominent VIP booth where they can eye the sequined wrigglers on the dancefloor as diners in a restaurant might a tank of lobsters. Freshness is guaranteed since no woman of legal drinking age would dare show her face for fear of being catcalled 'grandma'.

The Queenies and the Shays, having never been to England, take Rodney's at face value as a perfect facsimile. He's gone to great lengths to assure them it is. The bar, usually dotted with the latest London music papers, is stocked with Watney's Red Barrel, Newcastle Brown Ale, Bass and Guinness. Snacks include sausage rolls and Cornish pasties. All sipped, scoffed and thrown up to the British beat of T. Rex, Slade and Gary Glitter. All that's missing is a doorman in a bobbie's outfit kneebending ''ello, 'ello, 'ello'. And maybe some better understanding that most pubs in England aren't honey traps crawling with 12-year-olds scrubbed up like hookers.

Tonight in Rodney's is no different. The Bass pours flat and The Sweet plays loud as tiny buttocks bump and bounce, studied by lip-licking Hollywood cowboys with Rod Stewart haircuts wishing for once in their lives they were Silverhead roadies all the way from Basingstoke. In wall mirrors and compacts, eyelids that should be drooping over homework quiver under mascara brushes, every so often batting towards the vacant VIP booth like huntresses hoping they might suddenly catch the arrival of The Big Game. Because you can hear it buzzing around the club almost as loud as the funky glitter music. Everyone knows. *He's* back in town!

They were waiting for him when he arrived by Super Chief at Union Station in the craziest outfit, his hair 'the colour of carrots'. They know he's staying out at the Beverly Hills Hilton but the rest of his band are down the Hyatt Continental. He's playing two shows this weekend, one out in Long Beach and another right here at the Palladium. So he's just gotta show up in Rodney's sooner or later because, oh well, you *know* what good friends they are as there's even a photo of them together there on the wall. And when he does, it'll be every chick for herself. Just like *Star* magazine says, '*a true fox is quietly and personally aggressive . . .*'

THEY WAIT IN VAIN. David never shows his face in Rodney's. He rarely shows his face at all, not after a bad night further up the Strip at the Rainbow Bar & Grill where Stuey the bodyguard earns his keep fixing some creep chucking cries of 'fairy' and one badly aimed fist. The few times he *is* seen out on the town in female company, the women are most definitely *women* and always a year or two older than he is: a cosy meal in the 'London bistro ambience' of his favourite restaurant, Lost on Larrabee, talking shows and showmanship over organic entrées with his new friend, Bette Midler, and attending the Divine Miss M's own concert downtown with another close friend and singer, former Ikette Claudia Lennear. The nappy-rash nymphets still jiggling their hips to 'The Jean Genie' down Rodney's can dream on. Given his menu options these days, David just doesn't much care for chicken.

'*TOH-REE-NEE-KOO.*'

'What's that?'

'Chicken,' says David. '*Toh-ree-nee-koo.*'

Somewhere in the brilliant blue North Pacific – glad not to know exactly where, glad to be off stage without a gold circle on his forehead and a leotard wedged up his crack, glad to be simply 'David' again and even gladder to be back at sea with his old chum Geoff aboard an old cruise liner on its last rivets of passenger service – he sits with a cigarette and a small book about the size of an 8-track cartridge with a soft red leather cover.

'*Whisky toh soh-dah-swee,*' says David. 'Whisky and soda.'

In another few days they'll be docking in Japan, and with the help of the *Berlitz World-Wide Phrase Book* he's arming himself with the conversational basics.

'*Ee-kah-gah dehss-kah.* How do you do?'

It is just the two of them, or just the two dozen if you include the Fania All-Stars whose frisky Latin mambos have been busting his cabin's stereo since they cast off from California after the last of his moderately few American dates, leaving behind him a lot of loose change.

Six weeks of satisfied lovers, including a waitress named Ava who hasn't forgotten his pillow talk about being hired as a backing singer and now intends to hunt him to the ends of the Earth till she is.

The respect of one Mick Jagger who came to see him play to 14,000 at Long Beach Arena, deciding 'I don't think in three years' time we'll be laughing at what David does because he's done it better than anybody else'.

One haunting mental snapshot of a twitchy Iggy with his new girlfriend, not yet 14.

One Campari-soaked promise to produce Bette Midler's next album.

One drummer currently undergoing a course in magnetically wiping his personality with the help of Garson's LA friends and the teachings of L. Ron Hubbard.

And the tour-end dividend of 'Space Oddity', the single, and *Space Oddity*, the album, both bouncing the right side of 'Dueling Banjos' and Steely Dan in the US Top 20s.

He also leaves behind one manager, now cemented to New York as Mainman's global HQ from where Defries hatches rumours David will soon stop touring altogether to focus on a Hollywood film career. A contract is being finalised for him to take the lead role in an adaptation of the cult sci-fi novel *Stranger in a Strange Land* about a human born on the planet Mars whose inherited extraterrestrial powers lead him to start a new religious movement on Earth. So he says.

It isn't true, but it sounds believable Ziggy-shaped typecasting, and enough papers fall for it to print David's name and 'Hollywood' in the same sentence. That's the whole point. Now to sit by the phone and wait for the calls from the real studio bigwigs wanting a piece of the BOWIE™ big-screen action.

'*Sook-kah-ree dah'ee-joh-boo dehss.*'

A thousand leagues from Tinseltown, it is just gone 3 p.m. on the SS *Oronsay*, David and Geoff's favourite hour, when afternoon tea will be served in the Edinburgh Room. China cups, smoked salmon and crustless bread. The simple pleasures of a man enjoying a few days' precious freedom not having to be Ziggy Stardust. More than he realised he ever would.

'*Sook-kah-ree dah'ee-joh-boo dehss.*'

For now, at least, yes.

'Everything is all right.'

FIVE

HE SEES HIS NAME before he's able to distinguish a single Japanese face. '*Welcome! DAVID BOWIE.*'

A giant white banner, corner-stamped with the insignia of RCA Records, flaps between two poles on the Yokohama dockside above the umbrellas of a rain-sodden crowd of several hundred. His anonymity evaporates in the mist with every nautical inch the *Oronsay* glides closer to the harbour. For two weeks his fellow passengers have known David was some*thing*, what with the dyed hair and those gaudy clothes. Then the rumours they had 'a pop star' in their midst began circulating among the shampoo-and-sets stabbing their peach melbas in the Argyll restaurant, having spied him pull up a chair at the Captain's table alongside the ship's more familiar celebrity guest, 82-year-old KFC millionaire Colonel Sanders. But as they crowd the railings and marvel at his welcome committee, only now do they realise David really must be some*body*. Because despite 70-odd Japanese branches of KFC fronted by his life-sized fibreglass replica, there aren't any banners for the Colonel.

Humbled, David waves and blows them kisses as the rain drizzles and the anchor drops. He's not reached the top of the gangplank when the first in a forest of bouquets is thrust under his nose, making a handy shield against the blinding camera flashes. The Japanese, in greys and whites and browns and soft blues, are tea ceremony manners and toyshop smiles. David, in his multicoloured jacket, burnt orange hair and eyebrowless face as pale and translucent as one of their gyoza dumplings, is as queer a fish to set foot on their archipelago since the first Portuguese merchant waved *olá* to a samurai 400 years earlier. He finds them just as mystifying as they greet him in infinite different bows, some with arms straight, others with steepled fingers as if in prayer, some from the neck, some from the shoulders, some with their whole bodies like they're bobbing for apples. Smiling and squinting nervously behind his flowers, David makes a few concessionary dips of his head.

'*Ee-kah-gah dehss-kah.*'

The half-hour chauffeured drive from Yokohama to his hotel in the heart of Tokyo is its own backseat *Star Trek*. Streets of concertinaed shops shouting over one another in signs of alien script. Traffic so tight that every lane looks like a necklace with tiny cars for beads. Fatso-free pavements heaving with perfect little people dressed like they're off to a doll's house in the early 1960s: shorthaired business men with glasses and briefcases, young girls in matching skirts and car coats clenching handbags in their elbows, housewives in smocks and geta sandals, schoolgirls in ribboned straw boaters. And every so often the rare flash of a flared trouser, a miniskirt or a Cuban heel as a reminder he's still on the same planet where The Beatles actually happened. Then again, the day David arrives, the number 1 song in Japan is a sad tune about leaves by a young woman whose image has earned her the nickname 'Snow White'. Perhaps he isn't.

Situated just south of the Imperial Palace, the Imperial Hotel was once so exotic as to be easily confused with the fortress next door. To its rebuilt shame, it now looks like any other expensive Western hotel, but the service is still silver and the foundations supposedly quake-proof. Whatever shenanigans rock David's suite, the earth won't be moving.

'DARLING!'

Angie flies in the following day. In one hand a suitcase. In her other their son.

'DADDY!'

David looks down at his knees and sees shining milk teeth, golden hair and big blue-grey eyes. The only eyes with the power to see what the rest of the world does not. Not Bowie, not Ziggy, just Daddy. A love that only Zowie understands. And a loss only David can.

Poor kid. If only he was *just* Daddy.

CROSS-LEGGED AND SHOELESS, David squats on a tatami mat at a long low table laid with an exquisite array of tiny bowls, tinier cups, bamboo baskets and flat patterned plates of every geometric shape. At intervals, a partition in the wall slides open and more tiny portions appear, carried by silently treading geisha-like waitresses in obis and kimonos. Outside, the burble of a stream winding through an ornamental garden of aged pine trees, decorative maples and cherry blossoms. Inside, the polite click of chopsticks and clink of saké cups, the smell of things that once swam and snorted now chopped into little pieces then boiled, pickled, fried, steamed and delicately laid to rest on pickled plums or floating in murky soups no bigger than a finger bowl.

The elite Han-Nya-En restaurant is set in the former mansion of a feudal lord and makes no architectural effort to shake that memory. Joining David for their reassuringly expensive kaiseki dinner are his new clothes designer friend Kansai and a cheery young man who David last saw in the guise of a courtesan princess being wooed by a fishmonger.

His name is Bandō Tamasaburō, a 22-year-old kabuki actor currently starring in Yukio Mishima's *The Sardine Seller's Net of Love* at the Kabukiza theatre where he allowed David into his dressing room for a beginner's lesson in the art of the onnagata – those most venerated of kabuki players like himself who dedicate their careers to the exclusive portrayal of women.

David sat behind him in the mirror with the eyes of a thieving magpie, transfixed as Bandō first rubbed his entire face with wax before caking on a thick foundation of white oshiroi powder: a blank canvas to blend deep red around the lids and cheeks, draw around the eyes, score on black eyebrows and finish with a perfect scarlet kiss of a mouth. Just wax, water powder and paint and an everyday he becomes the most exquisite of shes. Asked what made Bandō want to become an onnagata, he replies, 'Because I longed for a world of beauty beyond my reach.'

David blinks back at him and falls deeper in love with Japan.

It's impossible for him not to. In one of Tokyo's oldest department stores, Seibu, they've posters of David 20 foot high next to the main escalators. His first concert here witnesses a packed hall of mostly young girls shrieking 'Zee-gee!' as they bounce out of their seats as far as family honour dares, none of them understanding a word he's singing. David compensates with his actions, stripping down to a pink jockstrap studded with rhinestones and humping the stage, all gurning sweat and thrusting sinews. No translations are necessary. Such *'violent and erotic narcissism'* may disgust one reviewer but most are smitten. *'Possibly the most interesting performer ever in the pop music genre.'*

Yes. David is in love.

And now all of this. The bowing geishas, the aromatic ballet of the different courses, the gently stupefying rice wine, the company of his two new friends, Kansai in the middle translating West to East and East to West, the three of them snug on their zabutons, snapping sticks and sipping cups, discussing the endless possibilities of their respective crafts.

The plates clear and the saké flows.

Kansai, casually stylish in a silk top embroidered with a giant cat, is nowhere near as outrageous as the new set of stage clothes he's just made David: the padded one he calls 'Space Samurai', or the legless silver number with golden tasselled sleeves shimmering like 'Spring Rain'.

Bandō, tall, thin and boyish, short hair and a plain shirt, looks nothing like he does when a magnificent she on stage.

David, orange trousers, red hair, milky skin and those Siberian Husky eyes, looks exactly as he does when up in the spotlight as 'Zee-gee!' But then that's not really *him*, is it? Like he keeps saying, it's only a *role*. Just clothes and hair and make-up. He could take it all off anytime he chooses. It's just that right now he has no choice. After Tokyo it's Hiroshima, then Kobe, then Osaka, then Tokyo again, then it'll be back around England all through the summer, the dates already announced and the tickets sold out. Straight after that, Defries wants him to go to Europe – he's already got Dai from Mainman's London office in France sizing up theatres – then back to America for an even bigger tour, then maybe Australia, then Christ knows where else.

Because it's not like Bandō, who can wipe it all off his face and walk down the street as good as invisible. That's the uniquely Japanese way of the onnagata. Admired. *Respected*, even.

No, because David hails from the silly isles of Widow Twankey and Danny La Rue. You tart up once there, me lad, and they never forget it. That's why he's 'Ziggy Stardust', today and forever. Call himself 'Aladdin Sane' if he wants but everyone knows Aladdin's just David hiding behind the curtains pretending Ziggy's not home. Nah, you heard them the other night. 'Zee-gee!' David made him and now he's stuck with him, till death do them part. That's the price you pay for creating a phenomenon.

'*Sorehana ndesu ka?*'

'Phenomenon,' says David, a little drunk. 'Like phenomena.'

'*Ah, genshō!*' Kansai translates. '*Hai. Phe-no-me-na.*'

'*Genshō, hai,*' grasps Bandō.

'See, ten to fifteen years from now, a time will come when almost everything in the world will be seen as phenomena.'

'*Kare wa, 10-nen-go ni wa subete ga genshō no yō ni mierudarou to iimasu.*'

'Hmm. *Hai.*'

'In other words, say that there was a car accident.' David raises his saké cup to his lips, thinks about sipping, then lowers it again. 'Right now we'd feel it as tragic and heart-breaking news. But a time will come when it will just be . . . phenomena.'

'*Kare ga, ah, itte iru koto wa, jidōsha jiko ga tada no genshōdearu koki ga kuru to iu kotodesu.*'

'*Ah,*' nods Bandō. '*Kōtsū jiko wa tada no genshō. Hai.*'

'*Hai,*' says David, eyes swimming, and takes another sip.

Out in the gardens of Han-Nya-En, fluttering beneath the Tokyo moon are the strangest and most beautiful of moths. Each once a caterpillar until the irreversible metamorphosis of nature. Reborn, transformed, until they die on the wing. Unable to change back again even if they wanted to.

TONY DEFRIES HANGS UP and stares through his hotel window at the cityscape beyond. Anyone looking up at him with a pair of binoculars would see a face of stony determination, the mouth not smiling yet the eyes shiny with stubborn composure.

A yen for his thoughts?

Maybe the thought that only a quarter of a century or so ago all of this was mile upon mile of scorched rubble and thousands upon thousands of skeletons turned to ash. But now, in only a couple of decades, Hiroshima is a thriving metropolis again. Nothing can be destroyed that can't be rebuilt bigger, better, stronger. Nothing.

He has his speech all prepared. He has to handle his product . . . sorry, he has to handle *David* with care, especially since he upset him once this week when he told him he'd just dumped Iggy.

Defries had finally given The Stooges permission to play a single concert back in their native Detroit. The day of the gig they appeared on a local radio station where Iggy dropped his trousers and gave listeners a running commentary as he played with his balls. That night on stage he spat at the front rows and introduced a brand-new song he'd written 'with my mother'. It was called 'Cock In My Pocket'. Defries was there to see it all and what he saw he detested. This was before Leee was forced to fill him in on all the blood, needles and broken glass up in the house on Torreyson Drive. Being a man who likes to keep his vices within the limits of the law and won't even tolerate a whiff of pot in his office, Defries doesn't need any excuses to sack a junkie. And so what began in a New York hotel room 18 months earlier ends with a long-distance phone call from Japan. Iggy and the Stooges are dropped from Mainman and evicted from their Hollywood home. And *Raw Power* isn't even out yet.

David was deflated, but acquiescent. This augurs well for Defries. Because their next conversation, in a few minutes' time, as soon as David knocks on his door, is going to be of far graver significance.

Money. Bread. Dough. Lolly. Dosh. In the end, that's what it all boils down to. It's why Defries dropped Iggy. There's no fortune to be made in songs called 'Cock In My Pocket'. The entertainment business is a business like any other. Profits, losses, nets and grosses. The business of selling. Sex, escape, romance, beauty, art, a sense of identity, whatever it is the daffy fan thinks they're buying. Just as long as they *keep* buying. Remember the wise words of the good book: '*Elvis, as a product, is always in the state of being sold.*' So far that's been Defries's same plan for his product too. His only plan.

BOWIE™! BOWIE™! BOWIE™! Sell! Sell! Sell!

Until the numbers stop adding up as they should. That's when you have to call an emergency meeting with your board of directors and rethink your strategy. Exactly as Defries is about to do with David.

How to phrase it?

'The thing is, David . . .'

No. Too woolly.

'The situation, David, is this . . .'

Much better, yes. The situation.

'. . . is this. The tour, as it stands, is costing too much money. In fact, if we carry on as we are, we're going to start losing money. That's Mainman's money, David. That's our money. *Your* money.'

Kick him in the wallet, lovely. Then maybe explain a little.

'It's not the UK dates. They're good, they're in profit. It's these other plans for Europe, then going back to America in the autumn. It's just not feasible. The costs versus the receipts times the risks. The books don't balance. We simply can't carry on like this.'

By now he'll be reeling so keep on talking. Start apportioning blame.

'It doesn't help, all this business with the band demanding more money. Only yesterday I had it again from Woody threatening to go on strike if I didn't bump up his wages. We can't afford to be held to ransom by these bastards.'

Is 'bastards' too strong? Hmm. Woody did call David a 'cunt' that time. Not too strong, then. As you were, Tony. But then there's the Mick problem.

'Now, of course, Mick's a whole different story. You still need him, I know. But I think I've found a way. I've had a quiet word about renegotiating his contract. Launching him as a Mainman artist. A solo album. Keeping him sweet, one of the family. Mick won't be a problem.'

But he'll be wondering where that leaves Trev and Woody, won't he?

'The others? We'll carry on and do the UK tour as planned. The truth is we can't afford not to. But once the last night is over, that's it. They're out on their own. Obviously we can't *tell* them. Not anyone in the band, nor the crew for that matter, or they'll walk out on us now and leave us high and dry. So as of now, *you* know, and Mick knows, and I know. But nobody else needs to know. Not even Angie.'

And then he's bound to ask. What then?

'Then we carry on. Keep you off the road, out of the red and in the black. Cut the supply now and we'll only double the demand. Make another album, and bide our time until the right offers come in. And they will.'

Then give him that 'I've never let you down once, have I?' smile. And that'll be that. Because in the end, like everybody in this business says, it all boils down to money. The one silver bullet that could finish off a phenomenon as big as Ziggy Stardust . . .

Knock! Knock!

Someone is outside Defries's door.

So he walks over, opens it and pulls the trigger.

HIKARI NO. 60. The bullet train from Osaka to Tokyo. Out of the window on the left-hand side, above the stretching tea fields and flat-roofed houses, rises the stunning snow-capped triangular Christmas pudding of Mount Fuji. Staring at it, in every pane of glass, a different reflection.

Woody, like a cold anvil, hard and serious. Is he looking *at* Fuji or *through* it? Into the infinite horizon of becoming clear? Or into the near distance of payday?

Trevor, like a sad teddy bear, soft with worry. Thinking of home, his wife, his bills and how much or how little he needs to be happy.

Mick, like a card player who knows the game is rigged, sneakthief, sly and shrewd. But look closely and you'll see the sad ache of a secret guilt burning deep in his gentle bovine eyes.

Defries, like a Napoleonic general, cool and inflexible. His orders given, his troops on the march. The last battle now commenced, victory must be his.

Angie, like a paw-licking lioness, nourished and content, her young cub Zowie beside her. These past two weeks she's had David back, her family back, if only a fleeting mirage. The three of them together, watching a sumo wrestling match, visiting Tsukiji fish market, dressing Zowie in his own little kimono. Precious Polaroids of the mind, blurry with pointing fingers and laughing faces. And now another, of Zowie pressed against the glass making his own mental potato print of Mount Fuji. How long before their colours fade?

And David. Reflecting like a mannequin in a shop window, elegant and detached. Weightless with the fresh knowledge of resignation. The driver of a car that's been told it's going to crash, speeding ever faster. Faster than this bullet train.

There are workers in the fields as the Hikari No. 60 whistles past but none bother to look up. When you've seen it as many times as they have, the phenomenon wears off.

SIX

WE HEAR FIRST. Soft *rumble in distance, get louder, more metal. Goes* klikety-klak, klikety-klak. *Then we see. Approaching dark green dot, come big like a square on blank white of snow. Big and loud and fast and then slow.* Klikety-klak *goes* kliiikeeety-klaaak *and green locomotive hiss into platform like head of giant serpent.* Peeessssh! *And then stop, make big metal groan.*

We stand in loose line. We women in headscarf and thick coat and big boots. All of us wooden crate or sled by feet, full of good things. We not wait board train and not wait peoples get off. We wait just for train. Yes, just train. Wait for doors open and peoples come. Hungry bellies and pockets full of rubles for our good things.

Peoples from back of train, good peoples. 'Hard class'. Speak language, not point and shout and words not understand. Nice peoples know pirozhki from pelmeni. 'Is cabbage?' We say no, meat. 'Ah, then two, please.' And so, yes, and so good if only few kopecks. But front of train is money. 'Soft class'. Private compartment, nice beds, restaurant car. When platform snowy get rug rolled from steps. No slip on ice. Special peoples. Business peoples, tourists, funny peoples from West. Lots of rubles but very bad Russian. Always camera, klik-klik. *Many, many pictures of station. Yes, funny peoples but many rubles.*

Funny man now. Look like clown with red wig. Red legs and yellow jacket with yellow fur. What animal? Very strange. And only little scarf, not thick, and flip flop cap. No good in cold. Yes, clown, but funny smile. Funny teeth, yes, like teeth of big omul fish. Wants something. Cheese? We have good . . . no? Points bottle. Ah, yes. Good yoghurt. Fresh, straight from yak. Smell. You like, yes? He like.

'*Skohl-koh?*'

Ah! '*How much?*' *Funny man know some Russian. Have phrase book maybe. Peeesssh!*

Train hiss again. Funny man panic.

Kliiiiickeeeeety-klaaaaak.

Train groan and move. Clown throw rubles and take bottle. What is . . . Oh! Too much! Ah, but must get back on train. He run. Everybody run. Clown shoes no good for run.

Kliiikeeety-klaaak.

Peoples jumping, peoples pull other peoples, some laugh, some not laugh. Look, funny yellow man safe with friend. All safe back on train, good peoples.

Klikety-klak.

And away. Well, short but good, what you say, Tanya – some bread left? Nice and black, ah, it will keep. And Varvara, you sell lots sardines? Come, let us wave paka-paka to train now. Big serpent slithering off into snowy hills. Get quieter and smaller, then disappear. And then, just like before train come, we see and hear nothing.

SO MUCH NOTHING. Just land upon land covered with snow, and lake upon lake frozen to ice, and any evidence of human existence reduced to the occasional wooden cabin, stone wall, warped fence and tilting telegraph pole. Makes a man think.

David does a lot of thinking. That's the greatest gift the near 6,000 miles of the Trans-Siberian Railway has to offer. Time to think.

It takes six days and nights from Khabarovsk in the extreme east of the Soviet Union to the capital of Moscow, skirting the edge of China and Mongolia, ploughing through Siberia, along the bottom of Lake Baikal, then up into the Urals and crossing the Volga to the great plains of the west. The longest train journey on the planet isn't all tundra and silver birch. There are 79 stations with 79 statues of Lenin, floodlit factories and lonely dams, black mountains and grey rivers, midnight wolves and dawn goshawks, Eskimo-like silhouettes fishing through ice, sad staring babushkas and dedushkas, the plump women scarved like fortune tellers, the bearded men in ushanka hats, all mummified in fur, some being sledged along by animals even sadder-looking than they are. Enough to make the plane-shy foreigner wonder how anyone could ever live anywhere so frighteningly remote.

The faces on the food vendors at the intermittent station stops are permafrosted with the same diabolical unanswered question. In the great spin of fate's roulette wheel, some get born in Brixton, others in Hawaii. These poor bastards got Siberia.

Still, they do make good yoghurt. David takes a swig as another battalion of fir trees flicks past his carriage window. And carries on thinking.

A week has passed since his reflection merged as one with Mount Fuji in the window of the Hikari No. 60. Since then he's been on another boat and another train besides this one, all strategically planned to get him home eventually, and at great expense, without having to put him through the screaming abdabs of boarding an aircraft. He shares his small 'deluxe' compartment, once again, with Geoff. They have a single berth each, with a small table between and room enough, just, for David to strum his guitar without cracking his elbows. Slide open the door and he steps into a windowed corridor, at each end a bathroom they share with the eight other compartments in their carriage, all to-ings and fro-ings monitored by the gulag-serious glower of the two uniformed provodnitsas maintaining the samovar of boiling water for passengers' tea.

More out of boredom than hunger, David and Geoff make frequent visits to the dining car where the wine is drinkable and the food on the bearable side of adequate – boiled chicken, schnitzel wrapped in omelette, pickles and potatoes, fatty soups smelling of vinegar and bloody red borscht. But it's more for the chance of new company and conversation that David returns. Sometimes a friendly cutglass accent from back home. Sometimes a pretty girl with enough of a grasp of English to be invited to his cabin to inspect his new art books by Tadanori Yokoo and to teach him '*doo-shen-ka*' means 'darling' in Russian.

But more often Bob, the 63-year-old New Yorker who's writing an article about the famous railway journey for an American news service. David has already woven himself into Bob's body-copy with tales of his travels since leaving Japan, where his last concert ended in a riot like

'Beatlemania all over again'. Of his passage to the Soviet Union aboard a Russian liner where he gatecrashed the cabaret and performed 'Space Oddity' for the delighted passengers and crew. Of his intention to record his next album in Japan, and to be the first Western rock star to play concerts in Moscow and Peking. Of how he thinks all his success was fated to happen. 'And it has.'

At his carriage window, mouth claggy with yoghurt, David is still thinking. In one week he will be back home where *Aladdin Sane* has just been released. Thanks to Defries and RCA's aggressive sales drive stipulating any shop stocking it has to pre-order a minimum of 25 copies, the album's already been certified gold before the first till rings. This weekend, it will enter the charts at number 1. Its trailer single, 'Drive-In Saturday', will have risen to number 3. In another fortnight his next tour will commence in London with his biggest UK concert to date in front of 18,000 fans at Earl's Court, every seat sold out. And all this has happened while David has been on the other side of the world. On stage causing riots in a pink jockstrap. At sea, serenading drunk Russians somewhere in the Pacific. And here, chugging through the lost latitudes of Siberia, his muse the endless tableau of solitude and *klikety-klak*. Enjoying the rare sensation, for as long as it lasts, of being watched by absolutely no one.

HE IS WATCHED by absolutely everyone. Hundreds mill through Red Square from every direction and all twist their heads, slow their pace or stop dead on the cobbles to take an eyeful of David.

Not any old eyeful. A very specific Muscovite eyeful. An eyeful that wonders whether to report this sighting of an obvious dissident to the KGB, or whether failing to do so will itself mean being woken at 4 a.m. by the pressure of a Makarov silencer poking against their temple. As it is, some of those watching him are already in military uniform and as many who are wearing plain overcoats have the faces of men who don't flinch at the sound of screams and fizzing electrodes.

The problem is the same problem David has anywhere else, which is the problem of not looking like anyone else, which itself hasn't really been a problem for most of the 5,000 miles of the Trans-Siberian Express. In Moscow it's definitely a problem, even if with his red hair, orange trousers and the favourite yellow fur bomber jacket he's been wearing all week he's no more colourful than the Neapolitan ice cream domes of St Basil's Cathedral straight in front of them. But then they're domes. David's a Western tourist. A very, very conspicuous Western tourist.

The dossier-typing eyes continue to follow him as he, Geoff and his new friend Bob the American newsman shuffle away from the queues for Lenin's tomb and over to the other side of the square, seeking shelter in the imposingly grand GUM shopping arcade, an architectural relic of Tsarist Russia which despite sharing the splendour of a Viennese palace and the skylight of a Victorian palm house still manages to feel like Alcatraz. But then this is Moscow. It's not just the people, it's the air itself. Every breath is like a leather glove on the shoulder. David is nevertheless determined that, when in Russia, do as the Ruskies do, and so leads the way to a worker's cafeteria where he hopes to better understand the country through its cuisine. One gagging forkful of jellied meatball slithering on grey cabbage and he's reminded why he'd make a lousy communist.

Tomorrow will be May Day, and all around Red Square the hammers and sickles are already flapping on the flagpoles ready for President Brezhnev and the big parade. David will watch most of it from his brutal concrete and glass breezeblock of a hotel just over the road on the corner of Gorky Street. Since it opened three years ago, the Intourist has become the favourite place for Westerners to stay in Moscow, mainly because that's where the Kremlin tells them to. It saves a lot of time and trouble since all the rooms are bugged.

The KGB won't hear any great intelligence from David's room. Just the soft whirr of the cine camera he bought in Japan as he crouches by his window zooming in on the stoical masses celebrating victory in the war against capitalist imperialism. And the stray hummings and strummings of some new tunes he's been fiddling with in more inspired moments of deluxe class, cigarettes and *doo-shen-ka* kisses. An anti-rock'n'roll man like Leonid Brezhnev wouldn't be remotely interested.

ONE-AND-A-HALF THOUSAND MILES from Red Square, where the embalmed body of Lenin, the father of the Soviet Union, lies on his back in a glass sarcophagus in a stone mausoleum five decades after he died, the 50-year-old naked body of the Air Force Minister of Her Majesty's Government of the United Kingdom lies in a similar position beneath a candlewick spread in a double bed in a plush, Regency-furnished apartment in northwest London.

Unlike cold and waxy Vladimir Ilyich, Lord Antony Claud Frederick Lambton, warm and sweaty having not long ejaculated with a deep grunt of satisfaction, is very much alive. So is the Irish woman half his age sat up in bed beside him, lighting a joint which will soon pass from her lips to his and back again. She has dark shoulder-length hair, a slim body with teardrop bosoms and a stern if not unattractive face which has made her a popular and successful high-class dominatrix. Her name, not too surprisingly, is not Mrs Lambton.

The real Mrs Lambton, the 51-year-old mother of their six children, is only 350 yards away at their luxury art deco home with its butterfly-shaped garden swimming pool. At this precise hour she has absolutely no idea her Tory minister husband is getting fucked, flogged and stoned so close that even a woman of her compromised mobility – still recovering from a series of misfortunes over the last decade involving a go-kart, then a staircase, then an oncoming lorry – could hobble round very comfortably within five minutes: out and down the steps of 58 Hamilton Terrace, right up to the lights at the corner of Hall Road, cross and turn left, then right by the Vale Court mansion flats – my, they *are* nice! – straight on until the crescent driveway announcing Marlborough Court, press the buzzer for Flat 9 and then, 'Darling? Surprise, surprise!' Her venerated husband, too, could just as easily walk the same way back. But then being a 'lord' in title if not peerage, being a cousin of a former prime minister, and being himself a junior minister, a chauffeur-driven Daimler at the expense of the tax payer is *so* much nicer.

The joint is smoked to the roach. A glass of Scotch while he pulls his shirt and trousers back on, then a fumble in his inside jacket pocket for his cheque book. He tears and signs one for forty pounds, hands to his smiling whore with a kiss goodbye, straightens his tie and with the gait of a man who has been thoroughly appeased of all earthly troubles walks out towards the lift taking him down to his waiting driver.

Tomorrow, Lord Lambton will be back in the ministry, having to be briefed and debriefed about the Russians' nuclear threat and their continued propaganda machine against Prime Minister Heath and the 'decadent' West. His wife, Bindy, will still be at home. His prostitute, Norma, will still be in Marlborough Court entertaining another of her clients according to their desired threshold of sadomasochism. So will her teddy bear with its secret tape recorder, and the bedroom wardrobe with its peephole camera, both placed there with KGB-worthy efficiency by her hustler boyfriend with a greedy eye on the Sunday papers.

And one-and-a-half thousand miles from this enemy state of the sick bourgeoisie, the corpse of Lenin will try its embalmed best not to laugh.

SEVEN

ENGLAND! He sees it, he stands on it, he tastes it. It tastes of flour. And fat. And salt. It tastes of cold pastry and savoury grease. Four months trotting the globe longer than Phileas Fogg, and this is David's first taste of home again.

A sausage roll in a British Rail caff.

Home? Almost. Just one last train to catch, but his three-inch heels are already firmly back in Blighty.

To get here, it's taken him another sleeper train from Moscow through the dystopian wastelands of Poland and East Germany. Then a stopover in Paris, where the disappointment of a cancelled dream dinner date with his chansonnier hero Jacques Brel was made up for by Angie, there brandishing welcome kisses and the new purple jacket Freddie made him which he's worn ever since. Then this morning's missed boat train, followed by Kronenbourg and jambon baguettes by Gare du Nord while they considered their options. Then the next connection to Boulogne to meet a cross-channel hovercraft, which David almost didn't board when he realised any craft that hovers, if only by a few inches, is also a craft that *flies*. Then the Camelotian vision of the luminous White Cliffs through the window of the Seaspeed guiding his approach to the shores of Dover. Then platform tarmac, café linoleum and a British Rail coffee and sausage roll. And he knew he was home.

He wipes a stray pastry flake from his lips. And thinks.

A sausage roll. A simple bloody sausage roll.

How many sausage rolls have been eaten here since he's been away living on Japanese baby carp broiled in soy and Russian doughnuts stuffed with cabbage? Think of all those children's birthday parties, weddings, wakes, church picnics, village fetes and transport caffs. Must be hundreds of thousands? Maybe millions? He chews. He swallows.

He looks around, contemplating the sad sweet everyday Englishness of it all. Stainless-steel cutlery, unpatterned crockery, colourless Formica, salt cellars and women in hairnets and pinnies mumbling 'don't forget your change, dear'.

He sips his coffee. It is weak. So weak, he could cry. Not because it tastes bad but because it tastes of home. Still the same bread-and-jam England of shit coffee and sausage rolls he left behind. The strange thing is, he didn't miss it. Not for one second. But now he's back, it feels like all those seconds he should have missed it have struck all at once in a paralysis of lost time.

He lowers his head to take another bite.

The bitten end looks back at him like a gaping mouth. Like it's talking to him. Like it's asking him a question.

'*What is it, David? What's on your mind?*'

He looks down at it, gulping, uncertain whether to answer.

'*Go on,*' it says. '*A problem shared?*'

He tries to speak. Does he speak?

Yes. He speaks.

He says, 'This is all a bit much.'

'*What is?*' it asks. '*Me?*'

'No,' says David. 'I mean, yes. I mean, it's all of it. It's you. It's this. It's everything, coming back here again.'

'*Why? Has it changed?*'

'No, it hasn't, but I have. I've been going through a whole lot of changes. They all started happening on my way back from Japan. I've seen life, *real* life, and I think I know who's controlling this damned world. It's like something out of George Orwell. And after what I've seen of the state of it, I've never been so scared in my life.'

'*So aren't you happy to be back safe?*'

'God, yes! Here ten minutes and I'm already starting to feel British again. I'm sick of being like Gulliver. Four months of America, Japan, Siberia, Moscow. I just want to bloody well go home to Beckenham and watch the telly.'

'*And just be you again?*'

'Yes.'

'*And who are you?*'

'I'm . . . David Bowie.'

'*You had to think about it?*'

'Because I feel like a Dr Frankenstein. There's David Bowie and there's Ziggy Stardust.'

'*And who is Ziggy?*'

'Ziggy is my ego. I created him and I created a monster. I went on stage and I became Ziggy on stage. I really did. But although Ziggy follows David Bowie very closely, we are two different people.'

'*So where is Ziggy now?*'

'He's here, eating a sausage roll.'

'*And where's David Bowie?*'

'He's eating the other half. Look. See those girls?'

'*Which ones?*'

'There, peering at us through the window.'

'*Oh, them? Yes, they love you, don't they.*'

'And I love them. I spoke to them just now. Signed some autographs. Salt of the earth, those girls. Because you know they don't sit each night and compare notes of groups, criticising lyrics, asking if it's valid. They just play the record. And maybe dance. It's all so pure for them. I love them dearly.'

'*And did they meet David or Ziggy?*'

'They met both. They met whoever they wanted to meet. A pop star. A man from outer space. The boy next door in a purple jacket. A fucking weirdo with red hair and no eyebrows.'

'*Which one are you?*'

'None of them, but that's not the point. The point is that this shouldn't be happening in their lives. I live on a stage, in their radio, in their magazines, on their bedroom wall. They don't ever think they're going to meet Ziggy at a train station in Kent. Can't you see? That's why it's all so bloody sad.'

'*Are you drunk?*'

'A little. I've been drinking beer all the way since Paris.'

'*Which is why you're having a conversation with a sausage roll?*'

'It's not a conversation. I'm not moving my lips. All this is happening inside my head.'

'*OK. Then ask yourself – what's so bloody sad?*'

'This. Them. *Life*. Because it doesn't really matter if I'm Ziggy anymore or not. I'll always be David Bowie. And I can't change that. I can't unperson him. And the day will come when David Bowie will no longer be able to sit in a railway caff eating a sausage roll. That day may be tomorrow. It might even be today. This could be it. You could be my last.'

'*But isn't that what you always wanted? To be a star?*'

'No, to be a writer. Music is just the means I've chosen to convey my ideas to a mass audience. David Bowie is a writer.'

'*So what's Ziggy?*'

'A character written and performed by David Bowie.'

'*So you're also a performer?*'

'Yes, but performing I find a great strain. Only now I have to carry on with what I've started. There's nothing else for me to do.'

'*The way you put it sounds so fatalistic.*'

'Does it? I didn't mean to. Really, I don't have a death wish. Although the very fact that I say that means the thought enters my mind.'

'*David's mind or Ziggy's?*'

'Both. Anyway, like I was saying before, I've changed. I'm not who I was. I don't really think I'm Ziggy anymore.'

'*Then what are you?*'

'A more mature David Bowie. More aware, more in control of myself.'

'*You don't sound it.*'

'That's the French beer. Or maybe I really *am* a lad insane. Oh, Christ! Maybe this time I finally have gone fucking mad. What do you think?'

'*Don't ask me, mate. You're the one talking to a sausage roll.*'

David blinks. Opening his eyes, he sees the bitten end still staring up at him. Dead and cold and meaty and flaky.

He takes another bite and hears nothing but the muscles in his jaw.

★

55

A SLOW, SLOW TRAIN TO LONDON. David, now sipping from a can of Skol, is not alone. He has Angie, and some of his friends from Mainman who met him in Paris, including his livewire American publicist Cherry, there to chaperone two rival duos from the British music press, each trying to outmanoeuvre the other in the first 'exclusive' homecoming interview with David. From the *NME*, an American photographer named Joe and a familiarly intense young man with a scruffy afro and even scruffier teeth wearing a tusk pendant beneath a denim jacket pinned with a single Jeff Beck badge: his name is Charles and such is his editorial monopoly on David over the last six months that he's already earned the not-unbitchy office epithet of 'Bowie's representative on Earth'. From the *Melody Maker*, the almost-as-familiar doctor's bag plastered with tour stickers rattling with the spare lenses of Barrie, and his accomplice Roy who, much like his prose, comes wrapped in a velvet jacket with a fedora on top. Between David's steadily drinking generosity and Angie's effortless powers of arbitration, everyone gets their pictures and both writers get their 'scoop'. The rings pull, the fags light, and the Kent sun sets over merrie meadowy England. All is blissful aboard the 6.50 from Sandwich, via Dover, rolling homeward to Charing Cross . . .

SEVEN THIRTY-THREE P.M. Victoria Station. Always busy as the weekend begins with comings, goings and passing diners sampling its new Europa Bistro with wicker chairs, Mucha prints and a decent glass of vin de table for 16p. But this Friday night it's much busier than usual. Teenagers. At least a hundred, and over half of them girls. They wear duffel coats, sheepskin collars, stripey tops, polka-dots, clogs, trainers, knee boots, denim jackets with 'Keep On Truckin'' patches and T-shirts displaying everything from *Super Fly* to Snagglepuss. At this precise point in human evolution, the collective noun for such gatherings might be 'an Osmonds' worth', or maybe 'a Cassidy's'. But as a handful of red T-shirts with the face of Ziggy Stardust plastered from navel to neck betray, this, in May 1973, is more accurately 'a Bowie's worth'. Every one of them here because yesterday the latest pop weeklies came out, two of which made a point of printing the information Cherry very deliberately leaked in her last press release.

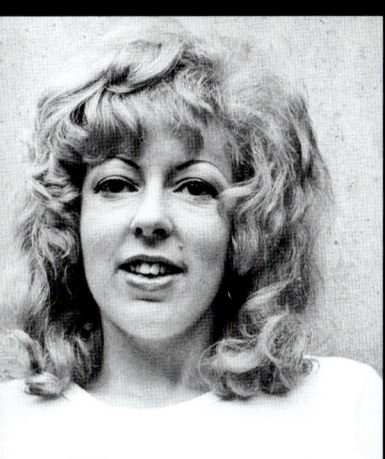

ROYAL WEDDING

NOVEMBER 1973

'*Bowie is scheduled to return from his worldwide tour Friday, arriving at London's Victoria Station at 7.35 p.m.*'

It is now 7.34 p.m. Which means, in one minute, a train will pull into the platform and out will step the fleshly reality of David Bowie whom no pair of young British eyelids have batted at for what feels like forever.

'*He will have been away exactly 100 days and since boarding the Trans-Siberian railway will have travelled almost 8,000 miles by train.*'

Away exactly 100 days. And now he's coming home, he's done his time, and here they are waiting for him, just like in that bloody song that's hogged number 1 for the past three weeks. All that's missing is one hundred yellow ribbons and an old oak tree to tie them to, like Pan's People did the other night on *Top of the Pops* while the audience danced their own ribbon-flapping conga. Oh, the things that have filled these Bowie-bereft eyes and ears while he's been gone! The gypsy twinkle of David Essex, breaking hearts and box-offices in *That'll Be the Day* since it hit cinemas last month. Telekinetic spookiness in this week's first episode of a new children's sci-fi show, *The Tomorrow People*. Newspapers full of this strange word 'Watergate'. Front-page pictures of a miserable-looking Lulu now that she's divorcing Bee Gee Maurice Gibb. Dreadful stories of murdered teenage Hell's Angels and '*Clockwork Orange rape gangs*'. Pierre Laroche, on his haunches, painting pretend back pockets on the naked arse of *The Sun*'s cheeky page 3 dolly Sue Shaw. And, crafted by the same French hand, a lightning flash across David Bowie's face on this week's number 1 album, retailing at a pocket-money-busting £2.38 when their red Ziggy T-shirts – entirely unofficial from a Humberside mail-order outfit still dealing in loons and joss sticks – only cost 90p, postage and all.

But now it's 7.35 p.m., and beneath those same T-shirts young hearts are knocking at their ribs like bailiff's knuckles. Because here's the boat train from Paris. And there's all the tired passengers pouring out of the carriages onto the platform. And any minute now they will see him. Any minute, yes, as 7.36 becomes 7.37 becomes 7.38 becomes 7.39. Any minute, no, as excitement becomes confusion becomes fear becomes hysterics. The last yawning travellers waddle with their suitcases out onto the concourse. None of them David Bowie.

A man slurping his lamb casserole in the window of the Europa Bistro stops chewing as he watches a red T-shirt slump to the floor. The head poking from its top is screaming.

'*WHERE* IS HE?'

STILL ON THE 6.50 from Sandwich, via Dover, to Charing Cross. In his head, a fuzzy soaking of canned lager. In his mouth, the next in a chain of cigarettes. In his lap, a copy of today's *Evening Standard*.

So what else has he missed these past hundred days? The Home Secretary wants to tighten laws on replica guns after some terrible business where the police shot dead two young Asians both bearing metal toy pistols costing 56p from Woolworths. War on ticket touts for tomorrow's Wembley Cup Final. An off-duty policeman killed by an elm tree in Finchley. Crimplene trouser suits, just £6.50 from C&A. Let's go into Europe with British Caledonian. What's on at the pictures? Malcolm McDowell in *O Lucky Man!* The fastest chop in the East, *King Boxer*. Super hood, super high, super dude, *Super Fly*. And the same old cartoons, cryptic crosswords and horoscopes by Katina. David can't resist reading Capricorn.

'*If you have much to do with young people, this should be a particularly stimulating weekend for you. Your thoughts turn back to the past this Saturday, but new experiences and fresh surroundings will be preferable to reviving former interests or revisiting former haunts.*'

The train jolts on.

NINE MINUTES PAST NINE. Charing Cross Station. Here's *Super Fly*, and Snagglepuss, and 'Keep On Truckin'', and several Ziggy Stardusts wrinkling on red cotton. All it took was a very helpful Tannoy announcement at Victoria, a panicked stampede to the Tube, three stops on the Circle Line, another mad pelt up Villiers Street and the gang's all here. In another minute, so will David Bowie, arriving on the 6.50 from Sandwich, via Dover.

And, right on time, here it comes now, grinding into the station.

And there go Snagglepuss and friends, vaulting the barriers of platform 5 to greet it.

And here gulp the Adam's apples beneath three peaked caps of the British transport police and a lone bobby's helmet, suddenly realising they're outnumbered about thirty to one.

And there click the first carriage doors as frowning unfamous heads peer out at the galloping throng.

And here clicks another, and out slips a man with red hair in a purple and silver jacket carrying a small leather satchel.

And there shivers the poor fox among the braying hounds as they crush him against the side of the train: pens waving, fingers pinching, his jacket tearing, police gloves shoving, peaked caps knocking, elbows digging, girls weeping, boys punching, lungs squeezing, feet tripping and stumbling between train and platform down onto the tracks. And all anyone can hear between the squealing and shrieking and blubbing and puffing is 'DAVID! DAVID! DAVID!'

But is it David? Only in body. His mind switched off the moment he stepped out of the carriage and into the opening credits of *A Hard Day's Night*. Because all that's left on Charing Cross Station, platform 5, is a head lockjawed in terror and a pair of legs running on automatic. And a stomach sickly sloshing with beer and one undigested sausage roll.

EIGHT

THE ICING ON THE CAKE is white with a red and blue lightning flash. The piped lettering reads, 'WELCOME HOME ALADDIN SANE'.

It is Saturday night in Haddon Hall, and the joint jumps as it hasn't in a hundred days. By the foot of its giant staircase to nowhere you cannot move for flashy clothes, fine hair, cheek-kissing conversation, cold chicken, colder wine and endless champagne, all seasoned by the same fog of cigarettes hanging over hairdresser Suzi's Aladdin cake. From the front room a record player blares *Raw Power* by Iggy and the Stooges, just out but so far the recipient of only one review in the UK music press. But *what* a review. Of all the eyebrow-cocking poseurs in love with their own *NME* by-lines, it's taken a cheeky Jewish ex-beat musician from Blackpool to rave how '*Iggy and chums play as if this was the first and last gig . . . living for the moment, with no thought of the past or the present, they have come up with the first real rock album of the Seventies.*' The wise words of Roy Carr find kindred applause in the swinging hips of Angie, leading the Haddon Hall dancefloor with Mick and Cherry, all being careful not to step on little Zowie who crawls around their heels fondling popped corks.

Over there, Freddie and his best friend Daniella, now living here as Angie's helper and Zowie's nanny, with her vivid new lemon-yellow hair. Wendy from the Sombrero, elegant as ever in a swish Ossie Clark for Radley. David's old flame, singer Dana Gillespie, busting out with her new 'date', another old friend, composer Lionel Bart. His record plugger Anya with her friend Chelita, sharing powder and lipsticks with Lindsay Kemp and his blind friend Jack. There's – my God! – there's *Tony*! Not Defries but Visconti, David's old producer who he hasn't seen since . . . ? Is it really *three* years since they walked out of one another's lives on the corner of Regent Street? But here he is, walking back in again with his new wife, Welsh singer Mary Hopkin, looking happy to be back in the house he too once called home. Burying the hatchet as easily as Suzi cuts the cake.

And over there in the light, the centre of everyone's gravity. Not 24 hours back under his own silver ceiling, David is tired but relaxed in loose red and yellow satin, eyeballs overloading with the shock of so many faces he hasn't seen in an age. And some he's never seen.

Now who's this? A face David doesn't know. Not a face anyone would notice straight away. But then that is one of its owner's greatest strengths. The power of near invisibility.

The face of a young woman in her mid-twenties with mousy hair, beady eyes, a wide nose and mouth with thin lips and minimal make-up. She wears a plain sweater and a long denim skirt, which between all the wild Cherries and Chelitas and yellow-haired Daniellas makes her so inconspicuous as to almost be conspicuous. But only almost.

She's here with the rest of Mainman's now ancillary London office in Chelsea where she's been temping since February. Born in New York, educated in Europe and fluent in several languages, she was by far the brightest candidate who answered their ad in the *Evening Standard* for a general 'Girl Friday', a term the coming sex discrimination bill will soon make illegal. Her duties to begin with were mostly helping the secretary of David's official fan club keep up with the growing hillock of mail bags. The first week, the office manager, Hugh, found her to be incredibly organised. By the second, startlingly efficient. By the end of the third, no less than indispensable, as if any formative memory of how things ran at Gunter Grove for the six months or so before she arrived had been entirely erased. And all of this she's achieved without raising a voice, slamming a phone or stepping on a single toe. Yet.

All that's been missing in her short employment so far is to meet the man without whom there wouldn't be an office needing her in the first place. Coming her way right now, where she stands with the office staff he already recognises. She lets one of them supply the polite introduction.

'David, this is Corinne. She's just joined us.'

He smiles.

'Hello, Corinne.'

And embraces her, as he embraces everyone.

Back by the front room, Angie is still gyrating to Iggy, grinning in delight, enjoying the moment. Perhaps best that she does. Because even if she was bothered to look over at her husband, all she'd see is him hugging that nice new girl she's already met in the office. Pretty smart cookie she seemed too but – hell! – *awfully* dowdy-looking.

So dance on, Angie. Dance, dance, dance like the music's never going to stop.

THE ICING ON THE ICING ON THE CAKE. It's not enough that David has the number 1 album, outselling the latest Led Zeppelin, the Faces, Pink Floyd, Alice Cooper, Roxy Music and two new compilations by The Beatles. Nor that his 'Drive-In Saturday' is still in the Top 3 singles. Nor that this week you'll find him on the covers of both *Melody Maker* and *Gay News*. That's not the icing on the icing. That's not even the cake.

The cake is four-and-a-half hectares of reinforced concrete and steel squatting between Kensington and Chelsea, its drab but daunting exterior that of a Ministry from *Nineteen Eighty-Four*. Inside is 41,800 square metres of agoraphobia priding itself on being 'the biggest indoor venue in Europe'. Back in July 1939, fascist toff Oswald Mosley hired it for a 'Britain First' rally, using a giant stage decorated with a lightning zigzag insignia. These days, it's more popular as an echoey cowshed where men go to ogle semi-naked women they wish they could sleep with, draped over cars, yachts and caravans they wish they could afford. But now an impresario from Devon has obtained its first exclusive use as a live entertainment venue. Big enough to hold 18,000 fans – making it the largest indoor concert hall in the country – the first act to play here would be making history. Slade know it because, much to their annoyance, they couldn't secure a date until next month. Nor could Pink Floyd, who'll be here next week. Which is what makes today the icing on the icing on the cake.

The day David Bowie becomes the first king of Earl's Court.

A Saturday. Forecast, dry and sunny. Exactly one week since London's transport system choked on the clashing reds, whites and blues of Leeds and Sunderland supporters kicking and jeering their way in the rain to Wembley for the FA Cup Final. And, once again, the buses and trains are choked with more team colours, but a very different set of fans. There's no ugly station scuffles because everybody's on the same side and, as far as they're concerned, they've already won. Because this is *their* day – the Glam Cup Final – and there can only be one name on the trophy.

Some of them spell it out in sequins on homemade T-shirts or sewn on the backs of denim jackets. Others spell the word 'STARDUST' around the rims of top hats they wear with matching sequined bandit masks. There are girls as old as 21, shaved eyebrows and food colouring in their hair, and as young as 14, veiled pillbox hats and chalk white make-up. Teenage couples wearing matching jeans at half-mast, and his-and-hers orange unisex haircuts, short on top, long at the back. Boys and girls of every height and shoe size with blue lips, green eyelids, silver cheekbones, scarlet boots, yellow dungarees, purple dresses, red T-shirts, gold headbands, Bowie badges, studded belts, single dangling diamante earrings like the one he wore on Russell Harty and an electric storm of Aladdin flashes crackling across every other young face.

They don't come in ones and twos, or even dozens. There are hundreds of them, becoming thousands as they squash into Warwick Road like a giant bag of Opal Fruits. In their jeans pockets, coats and shoulder bags, the tickets that cost them £2 for a stalls seat, £1 for the far gallery. Tickets they could now sell outside for as much as £25 according to today's *Evening Standard*. But after anxious weeks of striking off the calendar and fastidious preplanning of everything from nail varnish to knee socks – as if any of these sincere believers could dare turn Judas. Not one among 18,000. Who could never begin to imagine they're here to witness not a second coming but a crucifixion.

Not until they reach their seats, look around the columnless abyss and invent a depressing new parlour game called 'finding the stage in the aircraft hangar'. When they do, it is very small, very low to the ground and, from everywhere that isn't the first few rows, approximately 500 miles away.

A piercing earpop of screams greets David's entrance, but it doesn't alter the fact that for most he remains as vague a figure as a little plastic soldier in a toyshop window as seen from the top deck of a passing bus. There's a thin fuzzy rumble suggestive of a band playing through a PA system that's probably in the same postcode, but between the adoring screams and the impatient muttering of craning heads it's impossible to say what, least of all *who*.

Those closest on the arena floor try to rush the stage only to be battered back by a 20-stone bouncer named Fat Fred. Those behind them stand on their seats for a better view and, in unison, only succeed in elevating everyone's problem by two feet. This includes Alan Freeman, possibly here to bury David Bowie as he did Paul Raven, and evidently succeeding. And the assembled representatives of the British press, every music, tabloid and broadsheet here on a three-line whip, all of whom some logistic genius at Mainman has decided will best appreciate the evening balancing on a chair near the fire exit, ears straining as they haven't since childhood games of tin cans and string. An experience that could only be made more difficult if they were sat behind an Australian so cockeyed on Southern Comfort he repeatedly strips off his trousers and jiggles his genitals in their face. Which, as sod's law of ticket allocation insists, indeed they are. Even if the kids who don't leave halfway through in tears somehow forgive David, these nib-sucking assassins won't.

And so it's only the lucky few who can actually see the stage who have the chance to admire the new addition to David's minimal set. A hanging pair of giant lightning flash insignias. Exactly like the ones here 34 years ago when Mosley stood on a podium so high it hurt the necks of the 20,000 stiff-armed johnnies crowding in to watch him shake his finger while he ranted about nation and sacrifice.

'We will be true! Today, tomorrow, and forever – England lives!'

But that was the black-and-white newsreel then. This is the colour television now. Does England *still* live by flags and boots and funny salutes? In lightning flashes, knee-length leather and the stretching out of hands towards a glorious leader?

Don't ask David. He just finishes with 'Rock 'N' Roll Suicide' then leaves the stage, saying nothing. Letting the crushed fans sob, the house lights rise and the speakers wobble with his chosen exit music.

'Land Of Hope And Glory'.

DESPAIR AND DEFEAT. Their sentinels don't shatter him until the following evening when David takes a busman's holiday to Finsbury Park to sit among the audience of the Rainbow watching Liza Minnelli. She's been in town all week for three shows in three different venues, and whether it's the Palladium, the Festival Hall or dancing for the press around the fountain outside the Dorchester in a fox fur and 'my happy hooker shoes', Liza cannot put a foot wrong. Nor tonight. She is note-perfect, as is the PA system, and the crowd give enough standing ovations to constitute a Catholic Mass.

Everyone is deliriously happy. Except David, enviously ill. Yesterday's papers were full of how fabulous *he* was going to be. Today's papers are already full of how 'FABULOUS', in block capitals, Liza actually *is*. Tomorrow's papers, when his critics awake, he silently dreads.

He should. The man from the *Express* likens Earl's Court to an '*artistic defrocking*' in a '*barn of a place*'. The bigger blows land from the broadsheets. The *Guardian* calls it '*more of a cattle-show than a concert*'. The *Financial Times* describes it as simply '*hell*'. Twice.

It's been David's first colossal mistake. Even if it was Defries who booked it and Defries who was supposed to ensure it was checked in advance to gauge any technical problems, it's still David's head on the block. These first swipes of the axe will not be the last. Today is press day in the offices of the pop weeklies and the executioners' blades are sparking on their grinders.

Away one hundred days. Back just eleven. He can't climb on the next train out of England quick enough.

NINE

YOU CAN SMELL the harbour from the station. A briny, fishy smell that hits David's nostrils the moment he steps out of the carriage, same as the North Sea chill cutting through his striped jacket with the Lenin medallion he bought in Moscow pinned on his lapel.

Half eight in the evening, the summer sun not yet set, the concourse is quiet save for some six or seven canny fans who between them have worked out he'll be coming by train. They wait at the end of the platform, pens, notebooks and LPs ready, saucer eyes following his flash of marmalade hair bobbing behind the other passengers towards the ticket barrier, grinning beside Stuey the bodyguard who's already surplus to so small a turnout. The first to rush him is a young boy with a skinhead. David smiles and says hello. The skinhead replies. David doesn't understand a pipe-skirling syllable but sees the pad and shaky biro so stoops to sign his name. As his head dips, the boy can't resist a quick rub of David's hair, just to make sure he's real.

He is. Really Bowie, really here in Aberdeen.

Not quite as grand as its Tokyo namesake, the Imperial Hotel is only 200 yards round the corner, but being really Bowie he takes the waiting Daimler. He signs more autographs for staff at the reception desk, and again over a pheasant dinner washed down with lager and champagne. The friendliness of the pen-thrusting faces assures him any war reports of his slaughter at Earl's Court have yet to reach the Grampians. Or at the very least whatever the chippies wrap the fish suppers in up here, it isn't the *Financial Times*.

More likely the *Daily Record*, who've run a competition giving away a pair of tickets for all four of David's Scottish dates this week.

Or the local *Evening Express*, the sort of no-nonsense bugle carrying large adverts which begin: 'SHOULD HOMOSEXUALS BE RECEIVED INTO THE CHURCH? NEVER, NEVER, NEVER!'

David has two concerts here tomorrow. They should be interesting.

More interesting than the venue. Aberdeen is 'the Granite City', a claim it fiercely overstates almost as much as its intolerance of gay Christians. Outside, the Music Hall looks like a museum that died of boredom. Inside, it's left to a healthy throng of lassies in tartan scarves and woolly coats to sprinkle some much-needed colour. The rest comes from David, arriving on stage like a box of crayons, his body scribbling enough sexual suggestion to keep the advertising revenue of the *Evening Express* ticking over in screaming capitals till doomsday. Still not enough to move the paper's reviewer, a man called Ian who duly concludes '*his stage act isn't up to much*', and who will just as duly be annihilated as '*unfeeling*' and '*absurd*' in letters from furious Lesleys and Sandras hailing David their '*once-in-a-lifetime wonder!*'

Similar righteous apostles are still banging on the doors and windows outside the Imperial Hotel gone midnight. Down in its basement cabaret, the Best Cellar, David is in a T-shirt and dungarees gulping post-show champagne. As his eyes wander appetisingly through the smoke from one pretty face to another, his ears burn with a man from the *Record* asking how he feels about admitting he's bisexual. For a second David wonders whether there's a calendar behind the bar to doublecheck it's not still 1972.

'Look, baby,' he sighs, inspecting his fingernails. 'It's the way I am. I have no hang-ups about it. I'm not embarrassed − *are you?* I've always been an outsider, and I suppose it all makes me sound rather fey, but my audiences identify with me because I'm honest. I'm enormously sensitive, but they understand me and I help to fantasise for them.'

For them. With them. It is gone 3 a.m. when David retires upstairs. On one arm, a busty fan named Muriel. On the other, her butch best mate with an orange Ziggy cut. Both about to learn a whole lot more about his enormous sensitivity.

THE BAD HEADLINES reach Dundee before David does. It's Thursday, and the night train has delivered the London pop weeklies over the Silvery Tay to the city of jute, jam and Desperate Dan. However you take your pick, the news on the shelves of R. S. McColl's is awfy bad.

'*BOWIE FIASCO*'

'*Bowie blows it!*'

'*Bowie – an Earl's Court rip-off*'

'*Aladdin Distress*'

'*The show was a shambles . . .*'

'*Bowie at Earl's Court would have been good for fans who remembered their telescopes, hearing aids and stilts . . .*'

But the rooms have been hoovered and cleaned in the Angus Hotel where David and his crew are booked in for tonight. The Caird Hall is sold out. And, thanks to the *Record*, lucky Norah Clunie up the Hilltoon has won herself a free pair of tickets. *Aw, Ziggy! Ye cannae let her doon, ken?*

He disnae. The opening number, and David's not even had his wardrobe girls rip off his Space Samurai suit when Dundee goes fucking berserk. Then they do, revealing his skimpy satin costume beneath. Then Dundee goes *really* fucking berserk.

And then just like a poem by McGonagall,

That Dundee bard loved by some, but not all,

This Thursday night in 1973,

Won't be forgotten by the young of Dundee,

And the ones who didn't go will curse, 'Dearie me!

Why, oh, why didn't I go and see David Bowie!

That night he played the Caird Hall in '73?

I bet he must have been bonnie to see!'

Aye, he was, as even the *Courier* said,

In printed type they intended to be read,

'BOWIE WOWS THEM INTO A FRENZY',

And the *Evening Telegraph and Post* did agree,

His fans were the wildest ever seen in Dundee,

Since The Beatles were here in 1963,
And if only McGonagall had been there in person,
He'd have whipped out the book he composes his verse in,
And written an ode to match his best work,
Called 'The Night David Drove Dundee Fucking Berserk'.

DUNDEE'S BERSERK IS ONE THING. Glasgow's is another. A city so hard it'll crack your skull just thinking about it. Last weekend a gang of vandals broke into a Govan tenement while the unemployed owner was out, smashed up the furniture, ripped out the fireplace, kicked in the telly and hatcheted an eight-week-old puppy to death. And the Strathclyde polis still saw fit to blame *A Clockwork Orange*.

A cloudy Friday night and the city centre's pure steaming. The dog-murderin' heid-the-baws are still at large. The pished bampots are payday blind, yodelling ballads in wonky zigzags the length of Sauchiehall Street. The Tennent's neds are sharpening for tomorrow when they'll be training it to London, dripping with scarves, tams and tins o' Lager Lovelies hoping to hammer the English at Wembley. Which leaves the only genuine Clydeside droogies. The excitable sweet young savages crawling over one another like bees in a hive at the top of Renfield Street. Because growing up in a city where death comes as cruel and easy as tying on a football scarf or waiting at the wrong bus stop, life becomes a song to be howled at full volume. That's why they have to be *here*, in Green's Playhouse. Because tomorrow that wrong bus stop might be theirs. So tonight they're gonnae scream doon the fucking stars.

'WE WANT BOWIE!'

Twice over. Two sell-out houses, half six and half eight, with over 3,000 ramming in for each sitting. Not that there's any sitting. Just dancing and leaping, and jumping and roaring, and bawling and punching, and reaching and touching, and stomping and raving, and ripping and shredding, and breaking and beating, and crying and shrieking. Cast-iron seats bolted to the floor are torn up and tossed aside, their fliptop covers and cushions pulverised into confetti. The overcrowded balcony bounces like a diving board and one poor numptie breaks his ribs taking a splash in the thrashing laldy below. By the second house, the polis have called in squad car reinforcements while four ambulances stretcher out the twisted bodies. Eight kids end up in the Royal Infirmary, one with glass splinters in his eye, dozens more arrested, inside and out, including five wee weans charged with forging tickets. The Playhouse staff tell officers and reporters that, even for a Friday night in Glasgow, they've no' seen anything like it in their puff. 'Quite honestly,' shivers one, 'they were like *animals*.'

David thinks the same thing, but not in the same way. Animals, yes, but not beasts. Beautiful *living* creatures. He looks into their eyes as the seats and fists fly, fingertips buzzing at his feet like midges, hurricane hair stuck to their faces with sweat, his own hairs bristling as they chant his name with lungs the size of Hampden – and he *knows*. This isn't violence. This is love. Love of him, love of the moment, love of *life*. That's how much they feel it. So fucking *alive* with the music, and the noise, and the lights, and David teasing in his leotard, and Mick, bare-chested and bayoneting with his Les Paul, and the intense electric *beingness* of it all that they have to *do* something. And that something becomes a theatre seat in all its totemic obedience, uprooted by the bolts, smashed and destroyed in a symbolic victory of free man over cast metal. And to the ushers and security and the polis and the magistrate, this is vandalism, m'lud. But they're wrong. This, your honour, is expressionism. An urge as primal as that which made their ancestors daub bison in mud on cave walls. Just their way of letting the universe know they are here, and they are alive. So, *so* alive.

And so, so real, thinks David. From the stage it's like he's watching a newsreel from the Fifties about Teddy Boys rioting in cinemas showing *The Blackboard Jungle*. Except it's his fans who are the Teds, and he's their Bill Haley, the prophet of rock'n'roll. They believe his every word. *That we're no' alone! And we're fucking wonderful, man!* And David loves them for it. He tells them. 'We *love* you, Glasgow!'

But he can't tell them the truth. That what's rock'n'roll to them is just an act to him. Words and make-up and clothes and posture. A role he's learned to play so brilliantly that even shiteproof Glasgow can't sniff the fakery – but only ever a role. Because any day now, he's going to wipe off its greasepaint for the very last time. And for his sake, it's just as well these wild wee yins capable of Christ-knows-what haven't the faintest inkling.

★

SATURDAY SLOSHES in quarter gills to Sunday. In Dundee, the *Post* presses roll with The Broons trying to find Granpaw and Oor Wullie's sore tooth. In Glasgow, they're drowning 1–0 Wembley sorrows while toasting the plucky bam who invaded the pitch and walloped England's Alan Ball. And in Edinburgh, David is still on stage. His concert at the Empire Theatre couldn't start before 11 because of the bingo. But now the fat ladies have all gone and in their place skinny lassies squash against a thin metal barrier which is all that separates them from the focus of their craving lust.

Up in a balcony box, the newly arrived Angie gazes down proudly, just as she did last week in London. But the broken man who sloped off that doomed stage has visibly been fixed in the four days since she kissed him goodbye at King's Cross. Because whatever Earl's Court kicked out of David, Scotland has proudly restored. As it always does. As it always has.

Send them an Englishman with the wrong idea, and they'll send him homeward. To think again.

IT'S RAINING IN MAIDA VALE. Not heavy, but enough to turn the dusty red façade of the Vale Court flats a fresher carmine, clearing the gutters of leaves and depositing a glistening dew over any parked cars. But it can't wash away everything. And what it cannot clean, the lenses come to capture.

Scenes of a crime.

Scene one. Left-hand side of the second floor of the modern apartment block named Marlborough Court: Flat 9, where the deed was done.

Scene two. A fancy art deco-style house only a few minutes round the corner on Hamilton Terrace: number 58, where the doer of the deed lives with his wife.

Plain images of buildings. But when printed, dolls' houses for the speechless public to play with.

SCANDAL!

So much of it around these days, Fleet Street are spoiled for cover splashes. Last week it was 'BRIBES, THREATS, CONSPIRACY, SEX'. A dawn swoop by the Yard investigating pop, payola and the Notting

Hill home of Sixties one-hit wonder Janie Jones, accused of entertaining radio producers and record pluggers with hookers in exchange for airplay and rigged votes on *Opportunity Knocks*. Janie is now in jail awaiting trial and the pop group New World are wanted men. They even arrested singer Dorothy Squires, ex-wife of the new James Bond, Roger Moore, on suspicion of corruption; she fainted three times and detectives still refused her an aspirin.

But this week it's all about 'LAMBTON – THE CALL GIRL AND I'. The biggest stink in a Tory government since the Profumo affair, and on grubby newsprint not so dissimilar: a married minister, his prostitute and a potential risk to national security.

Lambton, the Air Force Minister, jumps before he's pushed on Tuesday with a 32-word resignation letter to Prime Minister Heath.

By Wednesday night, a full confession of his *'casual acquaintance with a call girl'*, his *'credulous stupidity'* and a picture of his now-empty home is all over the *Evening Standard*.

Thursday morning, and Norma's block of flats is on the cover of *The Sun* along with the fresh revelation that Lambton may have been on drugs.

Friday, and Robin Day and his BBC film crew find the disgraced ex-minister sheltering in his Durham country estate where he grants an exclusive interview to be broadcast later that night.

'Why,' asks Robin, 'should a man of your social position and charm and personality have to go to a whore?'

'I think,' muses Lambton, 'that sometimes people like variety.'

The breadth of that variety outlined in today's *Mirror*, describing the *'kinky'* contents of Norma's flat: *'whips, rubber and leather gear and bras with holes in them'*.

But do all these sordid details *really* matter to the honest working man and woman in the street worrying about lumbago, being laid off, the price of Jaffa Cakes or whether to bet on Merry Cricketer or Grey Mirage in the 3.35 from Newbury?

This is the question on the lips of Michael Barratt, host of the BBC's teatime magazine show *Nationwide*. His guest, *Telegraph* journalist Peregrine Worsthorne. The topic of discussion, this week's Lambton furore and whether the public actually care.

'I don't think . . .' begins Peregrine.

And then he says it. He actually says it. Live on air, on the BBC, for only the second time in British television history. From the lips of a 49-year-old ex-public schoolboy, stepson of a Governor of the Bank of England, one-time supporter of Enoch Powell and deputy editor of the *Daily Telegraph*. Named Peregrine.

'I don't think they give a fuck.'

TEN

IF IT'S TUESDAY, this must be England. And will be for the next six weeks. For David, six weeks of Post House hotels and breakfasts in bed. Crushed limbs, stage-door scrambles, kids screeching like herring gulls, clammy touches and undying love in the eyes of complete strangers. Pierre's powder puffs, Suzi's squirts of Streaks'N'Tips and daily repairs to fraying costumes. Cans of Skol, Coca-Cola, bottles of Libby's Orange 'C', fresh apples and bananas. Driven town to town by 'Jim The Lim' in a flash Roller like a cheating Air Force Minister while the rest of the band and crew snooze, read, play magnetic chess or nod along to the Stylistics on the coach. Grit in the bloody knees of the girls who chase after it, tumbling to the ground like the St Valentine's Day Massacre, and the elbow-linked chains of bobbies who never once succeed in penning them in. Backstage autographs for the blessed few admitted through the royal cordon of Stuey the bodyguard, 'tour mother' Suzi and, when she's there, Angie. Late nights in hotel bars of drinks, cigarettes and women – *always* women. And the knowledge, acutely conscious but never spoken aloud, that The End is in sight. All that stands between him and it is four dozen final bows, including matinees, in the cinemas and civic halls of 30 towns and cities scattershot across 20 counties, from the bitter-suppin' North to the scrumpied South. And in each of them a man, invariably, from the local paper who might otherwise be reporting on car parking, arson, rabbit poachers, the ladies' darts league or rock-hurling vandals, who instead must choose whether to swim with or against the tide of history crashing over their heads in £15,000-worth of lights and amplification. Scribes of the shires who will either Stokeishly salute '*a musical Merlin who leaves most of his contemporaries in the cold wastes of outer space*', or Worcesterly wither at '*the he-men, she-men and far-out tween-men*' come to hear such '*lacklustre music*'.

But if it's England, and if it's Tuesday, then this must be Romford.

And if it's Romford, this must be Stephen. At 16, he's already left school and working as a fence erector, which is how he can afford to spend £14 on getting his hair dyed Ziggy-red for tonight's gig at the Odeon. The tickets are all sold out, but he convinces another fan in the queue to sell him theirs at over four times the face value. It means *that* much to him – as anyone can tell from his silver boots, tight half-mast jeans and the askew zigzag scribbled over his face. An effort which, along with his new hair, burns him a couple of frames on the camera roll of the weekly rag beside two other fans: his mate, another Steve, wearing a starry vest and dungarees with a Bowie scarf trailing from the arse pocket, and a troubled kid from Stepney Green, here in the same denim jacket and red Ziggy T-shirt he wore to Earl's Court two weeks ago. For now, he calls himself John Beverley. In less than three years, he'll be known as 'Sid', and in less than six he'll be dead. Fame is vicious, and page five of this Friday's *Romford Recorder* won't be John's last squint in its glare.

On stage, David brings the sex, and Essex, the violence. That nobody is seriously injured tonight is 'a miracle' in the opinion of the St John's Ambulance staff, eyeing the balcony as they might a clifftop of lemmings, relieved only that the worst casualty is a stage-door bobby whose efforts to help David's limo squeeze away through the sobbing throng costs him a broken toe.

Tomorrow, the Odeon's double bill of Alistair MacLean thrillers will resume and Romford will pretend that everything is back to normal. But it clearly isn't. Just ask Stephen. Because what the dye did to his hair, the experience of witnessing David live does to his brain and 2,000 others. Seeping like ink into the wrinkly walnut gyri and sulci, staining the tender surface grey a hot bristling vermillion. And this tint is permanent.

★

IF IT'S HASHISH, this must be Brighton.

You can smell it in Church Street as the joints pass between the zigzagged moon children queuing up outside the Dome, where tonight they'll tot up £150 of damage after ripping eighteen seats from their mountings. At least four girls pass out, and not because of any dope. David ushers the wildest storm of unfettered adolescence to hit the venue since Led Zeppelin last December, and no sooner are the cushions restitched and the hinges rescrewed than Slade's audience pulverise fifteen more. The local director of resort services despairs. 'Some of these groups deliberately incite their fans to break the law and cause trouble!' But enough is enough. The blacklist is drawn, and alongside Slade, Zeppelin, Deep Purple, The Who, Lindisfarne, Osibisa and, more bizarrely, the Four Tops, David is henceforth banned from Brighton. 'For life!'

IF IT'S TV, this must be Bournemouth.

A camera crew from *Nationwide*, still on air despite the best efforts of Peregrine Worsthorne's potty mouth, is here to film a report on this 'skinny lad with a pasty complexion', who to their delight reduces young girls to puddles of suicidal despair should they blow their chance to molest him at the stage door. But if the BBC have come to stitch David up, the joke's already on them. Tonight, in the hour shortly before these sweet Dorset damsels frisbee themselves towards the Winter Gardens stage, millions of homes across the country are watching the *Top of the Pops* studio audience dance to a song David co-produced last year, now number 17 in the charts. Next week, thanks to this exposure, it will be number 10 – and the broadcasters of *Nationwide* still laughably none the wiser that what the words of Lou Reed's 'Walk On The Wild Side' are actually describing only a man like Peregrine Worsthorne would dare explain on telly.

IF IT'S CANCELLED, this must be Leeds.

David is supposed to play the university, but after a crew lunchtime inspection 'inadequate technical facilities' are blamed for calling it off mid-afternoon. By which time a 19-year-old sparky from Fife called Jim is already in the queue having been travelling here since the crack of dawn, as are dedicated fans from Dublin and Belfast and two especially distraught sisters all the way from Switzerland. Even the kids here from 30 miles down the road in South Elmsall receive the news with abnormal hysterics, and come teatime 'Bowie is OFF' is front page of the evening paper next to shock rumours Don Revie is leaving United. It's a grim night in Leeds, alreet! Amid tears and official Students' Union apologies, David's gig is tentatively rescheduled for the following Friday at the Rolarena, then cancelled again, then rescheduled again for the very end of the month. Yorkshire's parkin-thick patience wears ever thinner, and Jim from Fife has already had quite enough. 'I won't go and see him again *anywhere*.'

Far outside the city, in the restaurant of his Post House hotel off the A660, David eats a steak dinner, having just approved a telegram on his behalf to the national music press.

'David would like to thank the thousands whose pleasure and applause have made this our most enjoyable tour. Only 33 more shows to go, folks.'

It's actually 37, but the only one counting is David. And down.

IF IT'S LULU, this must be Sheffield.

She's here playing a week at the Fiesta club supported by a mind-reading act. Next week she'll be replaced by Larry Grayson. Presently divorcing an alcoholic Bee Gee, being 24 and newly single she emits a stronger musk of oversexed chipmunk than usual. If she's met David before, she doesn't remember, but she has, and he does: three years ago, on Valentine's Day 1970, at the readers' poll awards for what was then *Disc and Music Echo*; and again, last summer, briefly at *Top of the Pops*, occasions when David was still David and not yet fully Bowie. But now he's number 1 and she's a 90p ticket on the northern cabaret circuit, bar Tuesdays when 'lady members' can see her for 50p: roughly the same price as a large jar of Maxwell House. She still has her own Saturday teatime variety show on the BBC, and later this month she'll be parping 'My Ain Folk' on the other side as a special guest of Rolf Harris. But it's been four years since she last had a hit, and that was 'Boom Bang-A-Bang'.

'Another hit *would* be nice,' she squeaks to the local *Star*, just as kismet answers her prayers at the check-in desk of the Hallam Tower Hotel.

Because if she's looking for a musical Midas, in David she couldn't meet a better touch.

BOOM BANG-A-BANG! BOOM BANG-A-BANG!

IF IT'S CARNAGE, this must be Newcastle.

Tyneside means it. When the tickets for David's two performances at the City Hall went on sale six weeks ago, girls of 15 queued up all night, in the pelting rain. This itself rang alarm bells for a councillor in nearby Whitley Bay, as convinced that David's act 'could do a lot of harm' to the youngsters of the parish as they were that he was 'surely nowhere near as good as Gracie Fields'. Certainly nowhere near as safe. The first three rows of seats collapse under the crush of fans. Bodies gasping for air clamber for safety onto the stage only to be hurled back like binbags by the hall's vicious stewards as the sighing St John's Ambulance calmly crack open another box of splints. Two girls are treated for shock, and by the time the second show ends, the steps of the City Hall pant with so many exhausted and bruised teenage fruits that any passing grown-ups would be excused for their thoughts drifting to military field hospitals and a reminder not to miss this Sunday's episode of that canny new American sitcom *M*A*S*H* on BBC Two.

David, too, returns to his hotel in want of hot lips and, as ever, is spoilt for choice.

IF IT'S FANNY, this must be Lancashire.

Charnock Richard services on the M6, close enough to Blackpool, Blackburn, Preston, Manchester and Liverpool for its attendant Excelsior Motor Lodge to serve as a cheap stopover for touring rock bands. Tonight, David is at Preston Guildhall, losing his cool with more cavemen bouncers dragging girls by their hair. Forty miles away, Fanny are keeping theirs despite punctuated requests to 'show us yer tits!' at Liverpool Stadium. The female rock band from California who used to be called Wild Honey – changing it to Fanny in woeful ignorance of its typhoon-force teehee effect this side of the Atlantic, and yet to exhaust the innuendos of every spluttering sub-editor from *Disc* to *Time Out* – have finally stopped worrying about 'being taken seriously as musicians' enough to swap T-shirts and jeans for slinky bellydancer tops sewn together from $45-worth of American coinage apiece. 'On stage we get very horny,' says their keyboard player, Nickey. 'I've had more orgasms on stage than in bed. Sometimes when I come off stage I'm so fulfilled I just want to stare at a wall for a couple of hours.'

It is gone midnight when, buzzing in various states of unblinking bliss, their Silverline coach rolls back to Charnock Richard where the Excelsior is already in full swing. David's band and crew have commandeered the bar to celebrate Trevor's 23rd birthday and the four Fanny girls are most welcome gatecrashers. In particular, Jean, the spindly bass player with skin the colour of fudge and cascades of dark hair waterfalling to the small of her back. She's the younger and prettier of the group's two lead Filipino sisters, the one who says the least in interviews, the one whose face is usually on the gig adverts and the one who tends to elicit the most wolf whistles. Inevitably, the one David invites back to his room. To stare at a wall for a couple of hours.

IF IT'S HOLY, this must be Kilburn.

'Marymudderafeckingod!'

The violet-eyeballed drinkers in Biddy Mulligan's speak in tongues seeing so much green hair and face glitter parade up the High Road to the State cinema. Waiting for them outside are the usual touts – '*Bowie tickets, five pand!*' – street sellers with boxes of Ziggy T-shirts, rosettes and scarves – '*Two for a pand!*' – and even a vendor selling copies of *Gay News*.

'Befeckinjaysus!'

As the first pilgrims gather on the temple steps, their prophet pouts two miles away in a photo studio wearing his best ice-blue Freddie suit with matching turquoise eyeshadow daintily applied by Pierre. To capitalise on the tour, RCA decide David needs a new single, and as he hasn't one ready they've plucked 'Life On Mars?' from *Hunky Dory*, a song he recorded almost two years ago before he was Ziggy when his hair rippled down to his armpits. For the past month he's been playing it live as part of a medley and, according to Mainman, it's 'proved the high spot of his stage act' – even if by the time he shoots its necessary promotional film in Ladbroke Grove, David has since struck it off his setlists, tonight's included.

Otherwise, Kilburn is the same feature presentation of weeping and fainting, bouncers ragdolling harmless kids with needless thuggery and yet another copper's foot splattered under the tyres of the getaway limo. As the sweaty flash-faced freaks spill back onto the street, one silvery angel is stopped and asked why she's made-up so strangely.

'When I get painted up for David, I feel I am no longer me,' she says, 'and that's good, because I get fed up with being me.'

Through the windows of Biddy Mulligan's, men who forget they were fed up with being themselves ten jars ago gape at her with laughless mentholated smiles.

IF IT'S INJURED, this must be Salisbury.

His own fault for leaping off a 10-foot speaker stack one time too many. Nothing broken, just twisted, and David still insists on hobbling back on for an encore, visibly emotional, and not just with the pain. Something about the innocent energy of this wiltless Wiltshire crowd reminds him of the Spiders' very first gigs 18 months ago. A white-hot memory, more primal than Proustian, of a dying salmon swimming back to its spawning ground. He apologises for having to sing Chuck Berry's 'Round And Round' sat in a chair like a Ronnie Corbett monologue. Salisbury loves him all the more for trying. 'It's been a pleasure,' he tells them, then limps off into the wings. Tomorrow it will still hurt, but the show, both on the stage and in the sheets, goes on.

IF IT'S DROOGIE, this must be Bridlington.

The week David plays the Spa, they're showing *A Clockwork Orange* at the Winter Gardens cinema, and in the hours before the gig a gang of drunken lads from York assault a girl and her mother walking along the promenade. It comes five days after a Gary Glitter concert at the same venue ended with an outbreak of fisticuffs and the arrest of a young gasfitter for bovver-booting a kid already on the ground. At least David's tickets are a reassuringly civilised 30p more expensive than Gary's. On the

East Riding stock exchange that's a whole two portions of fish'n'chips, but he'll give them their money's worth. With scraps on top.

To those living just down the coast, 'Brid' may as well be Hull-on-sea, and thunders of young Bransholme Bowies have travelled the 30 miles from the home of Mick and the Spiders to see them. Among them, 15-year-old Gina from the Orchard Park estate, taken aside at the door to be told she's won a secret lottery as 'the 100,000th person to attend David's tour', the died-and-gone-to-heaven prize a meet-and-greet all-expenses trip to see him again at his final London date next Tuesday. Gina really wants to take her best friend, but as they're both minors she's told she has to take her dad instead. Mr Riley is even more excited than his teenage daughter. 'It's a once-in-a-lifetime thing!'

Once in a lifetime. Just as the girls in Aberdeen described David seven weeks ago. '*A once-in-a-lifetime wonder!*' But just the one life and the one time. Until the last grains of Bridlington sand trickle to the bottom of the hourglass.

What then?

ELEVEN

IT'S ALL OVER. He started it, now he's going to finish it. Here. Today.

Nice weather for it, too. A cloudless blue sky, warm enough to sit outside in a wicker chair in a stone-paved restaurant garden on the King's Road, surrounded by trellises and mock Roman busts. He's wearing an embroidered red satin waistcoat with gold trim and a black cape that he likes to flap every now and then to look like Batman. He saw something like it on telly in an old Hollywood film from the Thirties, so asked his friend Zandra Rhodes to make him one: she made him several. Below it, cream trousers, legs crossed, heels swinging. Above it, a wild bush of black ringlets spilling over a pair of blue and green sunglasses. In his hand a flute of champagne. He takes a sip. His lips twitch. It tastes good. It tastes like being Marc Bolan.

Remember him?

Possibly not. These past few months anyone would be forgiven for thinking he's dead. His face is still in magazines – a new ad for Elle deodorant where a giant can of 'Wild Rose' or 'Peach Blossom' gets you a coupon for his free colour poster – but then so is Valentino's now that there's a Sheik film revival in the West End. You don't see Marc much on TV anymore either, apart from back in January when he fried everyone's mind by turning up on *Cilla*. There he was, primetime Saturday night BBC One in his £50 pink feather boa from Harrod's singing a duet of

82

'Life's A Gas' with the Scouse gingernut, prodding fans to scrawl letters of protest to *Record Mirror* raging how the song was '*ruined by a rabbit-toothed man-eater!*' Then there were those TV ads for *Tanx*, the new T. Rex album with its cover image of him straddling a toy tank, its barrel pointing stiffly where his penis might be. Some papers called it '*obscene*' and *Valentine* magazine wouldn't even print it, but it didn't stop a seven-second commercial running on Saturday morning between *Sesame Street* and the *Osmonds* cartoon. Beyond that, only the one visit to *Top of the Pops* this year for '20th Century Boy'. Marc's Rothko moment – absolute simplicity, absolute perfection, rock'n'roll reduced to its two simplest colours: '*Oww!*' and '*Yeah!*' Not just the greatest T. Rex single ever but a visceral masterpiece of modern art. And like Jesus coming second in a Son of God contest it only reached number 3. Is it any wonder Marc hasn't played a gig in Britain since Christmas?

So where's he been?

Everywhere but UK number 1. Spreading T. Rextasy around Europe. Jamming with ex-Beatles in Los Angeles. Snorkelling in Barbados. Refurbishing a 17th-century vicarage near the Welsh borders. Buying a pony from the Queen's godson, 12 hands high, grey with dark spots, which is why Marc's named him 'Spotted Dick'. Finding a hedgehog and christening it 'Colin'. Feeding it beef to test whether it's a vegetarian. Trying very hard to stay sane.

'The Madness'. That's what Marc calls it. Three years, four number ones, ten Top 10 hits. Living out the lunacy of every magazine ODing on him, every new record being set up as another target. The way he sees it, you take a normal person's life: once they get over 40, they face the threat of becoming old, losing their looks, their virility, creeping ever closer to death. Now take Marc's life: working on number 1 singles, he faces that threat every three months. That's what it feels like. Every three months – like he's going to grow old and die if he never reaches number 1 again. And so it goes on. Until you go nuts. Or back off.

So that's what Marc did. Back off, to protect his marbles. And that's why he's here, today, out the back of Newton's on the King's Road, to share the wisdom of his sabbatical with the ladies and gentlemen of the musical press who'll soon be here gawping at him like a man feared lost in the Bermuda Triangle now miraculously reappeared. Greeted by a generous buffet of the restaurant's famed 'medieval' fare including garlic pâté, stuffed marrow, red cabbage and wild strawberries. And a champagne-guzzling pixie wearing a Batman cape telling them over and over again how utterly sane he is.

'I lie a lot,' he admits, 'but I feel my credibility as a poet allows me to make things up.'

So here's some garlic pâté with a fat slab of poetic credibility on the side. All the films he's yet to make, and will never make, like the science-fiction ones – is it three now, or just the two? – and the 'surrealistic *Alice in Wonderland*-type thing', which may or may not be the same 'raunchy' sepia silent film he's directing with Ringo and Harry Nilsson. Then there's the one where he's going to play the straight role of 'an elderly gentleman' which 'could be a Dickens thing'. He thinks. And the animated Japanese series featuring him as a superhero. That one might be called *Zinc Alloy*, but it doesn't really matter because he says they're going to dub on all the voices. Not to be confused with the separate American animated series featuring him as a teenage Doctor Strange type of character 'fighting the Monsters of Axos'. Or does he mean Doctor Who? Whatever, it's going to be like the *Jackson 5* cartoon, only hipper, he says, 'a bit more rock'n'roll', maybe like a T. Rex version of *Fantasia*. And let's not forget all the new music. The solo album with the Royal Philharmonic Orchestra. The album of spoken poetry. The one with him 'just playing electronic music'. And the new group he's formed with some black backing-singer chicks he met in America 'called Big Carrot', who'll be putting out a reggae single he wrote in Nassau and – *bloody hell!* – that one's actually *true*!

But none of this is the important stuff. Not this time. There's things he needs to say, that they need to print, that the kids need to hear. Not *what* he's done while he's been away, but *why* he went away in the first place. Why he had to step away from The Madness.

After T. Rex played Wembley last year it seemed there was nowhere bigger to go. There still isn't. Only Earl's Court, and look what happened to the first sucker to try *that*. He flew way too close to the sun and his wings melted. Poor David! Yeah, *his* name's bound to crop up in conversation. It just depends how Marc feels about him today. Is David still 'full of bullshit' and 'lost in the wilderness' like he told a German journalist the other week? Or does he feel sorry for him now after all those 'BOWIE BLOWS IT!' headlines?

He takes another sip of bubbles. Think, Marc, think.

Nah, Marc still digs him. He hopes David can hang on because he knows he's having it rough. But then Marc's always had it rough from critics himself. That's why he doesn't want to be a 'star' anymore. He sees himself more as an 'anti-star'. He says they couldn't get him to the London Palladium if they paid him a hundred grand. He's more involved with what's happening on the streets and always has been. He's an Eastender, remember. As a kid he used to work on a fruit stall and run around in gangs. He beat people up and got beaten up himself.

'I'm a street punk.'

Ooh! *That's* a good line!

'I'm just a street punk, b–a–b–e!'

Next reporter, and again.

'I'm just a street punk – and I'm much more of a punk than I was two years ago.'

All punk and no glam. Not anymore. No more lurex. No more glitter. That's all finished.

'Glam rock? Sham rock!'

What once was a revolt is now just ridicule. A revolt because Marc started the revolution. Three years ago this summer, when he made 'Ride A White Swan' he made the template of a bold modernist new rock'n'roll for the new decade. Quick as a Jean-Luc Godard jump cut from Memphis 1955 to London 1970, like the Sixties never even happened. The flash suits and the stars on the cheeks he only added because rock not only sounded dead, it *looked* dead.

'I just brought back the weirdos.'

That was the whole point. Glam was rock'n'roll for weirdos. Anti-straight, anti-square, anti-macho, anti-rules. Music for freaks, geeks, gays and strays. Music like a magic wand tapping the shoulder of the loneliest kid in the playground and telling them they're Superman. It belonged neither to grown-ups nor the past. It owed nothing to anyone the wrong side of 18. It was the roaring euphoria of ecstatic youth defined, and Marc defined it. Before David, before Alice, before Slade, before everyone. He just never, ever, called it 'glam'.

But now look at it. In the summer of 1973, what is 'glam'?

Glam is Gary Glitter telling the press 'I'm absolutely queer – for birds! I love women!' Glam is the tradesmen's overalls of The Sweet, who wear make-up today but, as Marc points out, 'if tomorrow every other group started wearing suits of armour, they'd start wearing suits of armour, wouldn't they?' Glam is Suzi Quatro, last year in the tabloids semi-naked with a bubble perm being called *'the Marc Bolan with boobs'*; this year in a £150 leather catsuit with a rent-a-Slade backing track that's got her in the Top 10, telling the papers she won't let her band wear make-up 'because I want my men to be men'. Glam is the laughing stock of Chicory Tip trying to get back in the charts by dressing up in superhero costumes and looking like fat wrestlers. Glam is teenage actor and *Mirabelle* pin-up Simon Turner releasing a drippy cover of David's 'The Prettiest Star' on Jonathan King's label. Glam is a magazine advert for Miners make-up *'for a night out with the boys'* and a picture of a girl flanked by four blokes tarted up like bad copies of Aladdin Sane. Glam is a Cozmic Comix parody of Seventies shock rock with a cartoon of a singer wailing *'Baby, let me take you for a sex change operation!'* Glam is an episode of *The Goodies* sending up the pop biz that sees Bill Oddie mincing in glitter as mock idol 'Randy Pandy – Superpoof!' Glam is some *Sun* readers missing the sarcasm when Marc tells them, 'I'm going to stick my head in a bowl of flour, stick peacock feathers in my hair and call myself Sibelius Sequin.' Glam is . . .

'Over!'

So there's your headline, ladies and gentlemen. Straight from the lips of the street punk who started it. Print it bold and print it big.

'GLAM ROCK IS DEAD! SAYS MARC'

TWELVE

LONDON WAKES with the thud of the paper boy, rubs its eyes, throws on its dressing gown, staggers to the doormat, bends stiffly, straightens up and blearily realises not only is it Sunday but also July.

The news is good, least for those following the drama of a newborn baby girl missing for five days after being snatched from her pram while her mum popped into a public toilet in Bromley. Two boys out fishing found her yesterday, abandoned by an oak tree, 'gravely ill' but mercifully alive.

London exhales with relief, shuffles yawning into its kitchen, switches on the wireless, hears Reginald Dixon's much-too-jolly organ, switches it off again, opens the fridge, grabs a milk bottle and, as it waits for the kettle to boil, spies a scavenging pigeon pecking the window sill. The kettle starts to whistle. The startled bird coos. The steam sings soprano. The pigeon flaps away.

Up it flies, circling above the city warming like a muffin in the morning sun. Swooping over high rise and high street, park and playground, until its shadow falls on Wimbledon No. 2 court, still recovering from its invasion of screaming girls last Wednesday, every one intent on rubbing their faces with sweat from the victorious brow of a startled 17-year-old Swedish boy. As the aghast umpire put it, 'This is the sort of thing you connect with David Cassidy!' The new

87

Cassidy being tournament first-timer Björn Borg. 'He's just beautiful, tall, sexy and strong,' trembles one 15-year-old 'Weenyborger' from Finchley. 'Much better than any pop star. I used to like David Bowie, but Borg is beautiful.' Even more beautiful than hunky Romanian Ilie 'Nasty' Năstase, the men's favourite until yesterday's shock defeat by an unseeded American college boy who put his victory down to his mum's homemade cakes nibbled between sets. But no play today, and so no crumbs for our pigeon. It drifts on.

Northward, over the river, gliding above the city, past Drury Lane where the hit Broadway rock'n'roll musical *Grease* has just opened at the New London Theatre to a tabloid outbreak of Fifties fashions and ecstatic reviews. Its star is an American unknown named Richard Gere, likened to '*a cross between Elvis and James Dean*' in his role as Danny Zuko, campus stud gang leader of the Burger Palace Boys. Except Gere, '*a serious actor*' at 23, winces at any idol comparisons.

'I am not a Marc Bolan or whatever. I don't want to have my clothes torn off me at the stage door.'

Our pigeon grunts, poops and flies on.

Westward to Leicester Square. Queueless before noon with the auditoriums still empty, their screen curtains closed, their feed and take-up spools static, their 35mm magic mummified in canisters like genies begging for the rub of electricity to once more cast their spell that 'Soylent Green is people!'

Flying on, over the rich rooftops of Park Lane, where on the ninth floor of the Inn on the Park, Howard Hughes fills another syringe. Three nights ago he actually sneaked out under cover of darkness, whisked by limo to a private airfield so he could indulge his love of aviation by piloting a Hawker Siddeley across to Belgium and back. He sat in the cockpit naked, as he lies now on his bed of paper towels, watching another old movie through clouded fishbowl eyes. Alone and unseen by neither man nor pigeon.

On the wing, over the Palace – no flag flying as she's in Canada right now – arcing to Chelsea, above Sloane Square where Upstairs at the Royal Court another musical only in its third week is already delighting critics with its '*transexual rockarama through the excesses of Fifties cinema*'. This being a Sunday, there's no performance of *The Rocky Horror Show* tonight, but no shortage of weird creatures milling about the King's Road as the first pints pour in the Rose and Crown. Homemade paper top hats plastered with shiny foil circles, others in tartan bonnets, splatters of Woolies glitter and W. H. Smith stars on their brows, baggy trousers and tight pedal pushers with 'Skweeze Me, Pleeze Me' stickers on their knees, long stripey socks, Budgie clogs and platform boots, Burberry check mufflers and tank tops embroidered in sequins with the names 'Noddy', 'Dave', 'Don' and 'Jim'.

Our curious bird cocks its head, coos and follows them.

Across to Brompton and up Warwick Road where whole battalions of them herd towards a humungous beast of a building threatening to suck up the surrounding rows of Victorian townhouses like spaghetti.

Earl's Court. Where six weeks ago David died.

And where, tonight, Slade will dance on his grave.

His grave, Marc's grave, everyone's grave. If 1973 is a war, then Slade have won, and this is VE Day.

Victory Everywhere.

Like David, this past month they've been touring the same towns and, like David, forking out for their fans' damage to the same venues. Glasgow went so ballistic for them they had to be smuggled out of Green's Playhouse in a police wagon and still couldn't get back in their hotel for the waiting siege of fans. And so they were driven to a secluded spot by the Clyde where they all sat with the rozzers in the back of the van. Eating fish suppers from a local chippie.

This, in a greasy newspaper nutshell, is precisely why Slade are the biggest band in the country. For all the glamour of Noddy's mirrored stovepipe hat, the castratingly tight gold lurex trousers, the altitude-sickness platform boots, Dave's cartoon 'Super Yob' raygun guitar and the sparkles of glitter in his hair, the raw essence of Slade is fish'n'chips. David and Marc, they belong to the stars. Slade are sons of the tarmac. The people's noize.

And the people's bubbles. This week they're number 1 again, and with their thanks one thousand bottles of champagne are popping in the homes of every worker at their record company and its pressing plant while they pop their own just over the road from where David shot the cover of *Aladdin Sane*. The Swiss Cottage Holiday Inn very nearly evicted them after the other night when hundreds of fans turned up, wrecking the electronic security doors, running wild through the corridors and damaging drummer Don Powell's white Bentley in the clamour for souvenirs. The next morning two schoolgirls from Camden who'd been part of the chaos returned with a humble letter of apology to the band and hotel management. These are the sort of fans Slade attract – as crazee as fuck as they are good as gold. And there's millions of them.

But only 18,000 lucky ones today, cheering and chanting on buses and Tubes from every London postcode, wiggling thumbs and waving scarves, others arriving like tartan armies on designated 'Slade train specials' from Brighton, Birmingham, Bristol and Manchester. Awaiting them is a new specially built 'Busby Berkeley-style' stage set with curving staircases either side, high enough for everyone to see and with the added insurance of closed-circuit TV projecting on a screen above. A deafening 13,000-watt PA system has been hired, with extra baffles hung from the ceiling to soften the hall's harsh acoustics. Everything David got wrong, Slade have righted. VE day goes off without a hitch.

Outside, on the roof, our pigeon sleeps. But not for long. Eighteen thousand young 'Sladists' roaring, clapping, fainting, chucking knickers, stomping their feet, pissing their seats and puking over the barriers with excitement wakes it from its slumber like the tremors of an earthquake. Squawking like a startled chicken, its orange eyes blink and its grey wings flap. A lone fluffy feather drifts towards the ground. And it is gone.

Flying a little further west, following the odours of hot fat until it settles not far from the river. There is constant traffic noise rumbling from the elevated Westway but nothing like the disturbance of Slade, and on the pavements outside the Odeon cinema it delights in stray crumbs of crisps and popcorn from the audience spilling out of *Avanti!*

Our pigeon likes it here. It stays.

MONDAY EVENING. Back in Earl's Court, Joe Frazier is taken to a bitter and bloody slugging twelfth round by Joe Bugner. One mile away on Hammersmith Road, our pigeon is greasing its beak in the bins behind Oddie's Café.

After yesterday it's no longer curious about huge crowds of kids in shiny clothes and sparkly make-up so pays little attention to the hundreds more clustering tonight under the Westway. But there's not nearly as many of them this time, and whatever's happening inside the Odeon, though loud and though definitely not *Avanti!*, doesn't rattle its clavicle with nearly the force Slade did. For now, this is still as good a roost as any.

By midnight the lightning-faced jazz babies have all gone home and the traffic is hushed to the occasional lorry and taxicab. The clocks inhale the first breath of Tuesday, and our bird sleepily watches as a British Leyland minivan pulls up on Queen Caroline Street near the cinema's back entrance. Two figures creep out, their silhouettes slipping into the shadows by the rear doors. Minutes pass, and our pigeon has almost forgotten them when back they stagger, arms loaded with what it couldn't possibly know were drum cymbals, an Electro Voice microphone and a bulky Sunn bass amp head. The heavy swag is loaded into the van, heads constantly twitching behind them as they shut the doors as quietly as they can, bolt inside the front, rev up and disappear into the night. Our pigeon pulls its head back into its breast, screws tight its lids and dreams of breadcrumbs.

Dawn, and another day of scavenging begins. Not so good in Oddie's bins this morning, and when an old woman scatters the ends of a stale loaf in St Paul's churchyard the competing flock is much too fierce. Dusk brings hunger and yet another beglittered mass rushing towards the Odeon. For the third night running, our pigeon finds itself cocking its head to faint screams and repetitive thudding vibrations. Until, at last, it stops, and with night descended again, out they pour onto the street.

But pigeons don't cry, and so ours doesn't understand why tonight so many of these young humans have mascara dribbling down to their knees, collapsing on the pavement in desperately clinging twos and threes, sobbing so hard they might weep blood.

And why would it care? When over there in the gutter there's the half-chewed end of a hot dog bun.

Coo! Coo!

Down it dives.

Peck! Peck! Peck!

Ignoring girls drowning by the dozen in puddles of glitter.

Peck! Peck! Peck!

The bun bounces further into the road.

Peck! Peck! Peck!

And all around it, still, the tuneless wail of the end of the world.

Peck! Peck . . .

It doesn't see the lorry. And it doesn't feel a thing.

NOR DOES DAVID. Only relief that it's over. He is otherwise numbly conscious as if drunk, which he isn't, though he's sinking enough wine and champagne that he soon will be. Quite drunk in an insane fog dream of colours, sounds and the faces of friends, lovers and liggers.

Here's Mick Jagger, his wife Bianca and Lou Reed sharing the same ice bucket. And Angie, Lulu and Jean from Fanny wriggling on the same dancefloor. And Ringo, Jeff Beck, Cat Stevens and Ossie Clark being shepherded into the same group photograph. And Elliot Gould, his girlfriend Britt Ekland and his ex-wife Barbra Streisand picking at smoked salmon. And Tony Curtis, Ryan O'Neal, Peter Cook and Spike Milligan trying to be heard above 'Honky Tonk Women'. And a 15-year-old competition winner from Hull with her dad collecting autographs from Brian from The Sweet. All here together in the Piccadilly slipper on the foot of Regent Street, the Café Royal.

Last month, this is where Paul McCartney threw a celebratory bash after Wings played their last night at Hammersmith Odeon. Tonight, David's doing exactly the same. Only, for him, the party itself isn't important. That's why all of it disintegrates in his prefrontal cortex like pictures scratched into wet sand, lost forever in the incoming tide of the next drunken blink. What's important is what he did, or rather what he said, on a stage four miles away not three hours ago, exactly as he'd planned.

'Not only is it the last show of the tour, but it's the last show that we'll ever do.'

And clunk went three-and-a-half thousand jaws. Not counting most of 'we', the band and crew, who hadn't been forewarned, who have wives, fiancées, kids and mortgages. And who are now either here at the Café

Royal sharing pissed prayers they'll still have some sort of a job come tomorrow morning or, like Trevor, stewing back in their hotel room calling David all the cunts under the East Yorkshire sun.

Odd, though. Because hadn't Defries already told *Melody Maker* as much back in February?

'*David may not make a British tour after this one for a long, long, time, maybe even years, especially if he gets into films.*'

And didn't they make it that week's front-page?

'BOWIE'S LAST TOUR?'

But it's amazing what people don't read. And even when they do, what they quickly forget.

As quickly as David will forget this party. He fills another glass to the brim as somebody at his table asks the time and is given an answer. 'Just after one.' David wobbles a cigarette to his grinless lips.

One a.m. in London. Glam is dead, and all's well.

ONE A.M. IN WOLVERHAMPTON. They've not long left Dix's, the nightclub where she works as a secretary, the pair of them now driving home together in his flash white Bentley. New wing mirrors and wipers after that mob of kids tore them off outside his London hotel at the weekend. 'Occupational hazard,' he calls it and she laughs and squeezes his knee.

Nine months these lovebirds have been together. Not yet engaged but her parents are secretly hoping. Maybe when she turns 21 in a few weeks he'll be there on one knee with the ring in his hand. But for now here they are, in love, in a car, heading back to his place on an empty road one hour into this new Wednesday.

Then bouncing off a tree, skidding and screeching 40 yards, straight through a hedge, smashing headfirst into the perimeter wall of a teacher training college. Crunch goes the bonnet, smash goes the glass and out flies the girl as if shot from a cannon. Right through the windscreen, up into the air, cracking her skull as she hits the ground. The impact kills her.

And almost him. By teatime he'll be front-page news of the evening papers and the hospital switchboard jammed with kids bubbling and bawling, asking if Don from Slade is going to live.

And, incredibly, he will. Not that you'd ever believe it to see him now. Lying here in the gutter, twisted and unconscious, as the champagne flows in the Café Royal. Just another victim of this bloodclotting, starless glam–dead night.

THIRTEEN

THE MAGIC DARKNESS of the pictures. The only light coming from a huge screen illuminated with flames and skulls which don't really move him, and flashes of black skin on dancing bodies which definitely do. The thick odour of clashing perfumes and colognes raging the same war being fought between cigar and cigarette smoke. And music, loud bombastic music blaring and banging with brass and drums and strings. The signature theme song to the film on the screen.

'*Live and let die . . .*'

The world premiere at the Odeon, Leicester Square, and every seat is taken. To get one you have to be the newly engaged Princess Anne, or the new 007 himself, Roger Moore, or his gorgeous co-star Jane Seymour, or any other member of the cast and crew, or just very, very famous like Michael Caine, or Peter Sellers, or Joan Collins, or Burt Reynolds, or Gregory Peck.

Or David Bowie, sat beside Angie, both dressed to kill with a mass grave of dead flashbulbs on the red carpet to show for it.

In held hands and synchronised smiles they are no longer pop-star-and-accessory-wife but now, as one, 'the Bowies'. For the last 48 hours their names and faces have been splashed across the papers in various stories about David's onstage retirement and the starry afterparty at the Café Royal, *The Sun* even giving Angie her own two-page spread showing off her legs, much like this evening's choice of split-to-the-hip oriental dress. And tomorrow, when the society pages report on tonight's Bond premiere, they'll be united in picture crop and caption as 'the Bowies' yet again.

Just as Paul and Linda are 'the McCartneys'. They've cancelled a Wings gig in Stoke-on-Trent to be here, which they need to since they're the ones who wrote and sang that bombastic theme song. Paul's attempt to follow the royal gala dress code is to come bare-chested beneath a tuxedo jacket wearing only a bowtie-shaped necklace. Linda's is to come looking like Linda, which these days means looking a lot like David: as even *Jackie* can't help point out, both currently have identical spiky-on-top-and-long-at-the-back barnets.

In his seat, as the gun barrel circles, as Bond shoots, as the guitar twangs, as the blood drips and an on-screen caption specifies 'United Nations, New York City', David sparks up the first of a packet of Marlboros that'll see him through the next two hours of hokey blaxploitation, voodoo hoodoo, stupid sheriffs, snapping crocodiles, circling sharks, exploding sofas and an utterly exhausting motorboat chase. Between the dumb dialogue and the soothing smoke, his mind forgivably drifts.

'The name's Bond, you have a reservation for me.'

Just like the hotel suite in Knightsbridge overlooking Hyde Park, as of last weekend David's temporary home.

'Room service? I'd like a bottle of Bollinger, please, slightly chilled, two glasses.'

Where he woke up yesterday, empty glasses and melted ice bucket, the sheets smelling of Angie. Before the week is through, on different laundry days they'll also smell of Lulu and Jean from Fanny.

'Lovers' lesson number one: we have no secrets.'

Nor they. Angie has her own lover flown over from Detroit, Scott, a mutual musician friend of Iggy who wants to start his own band and sign with Mainman. David has already offered to help him.

'Lovers' lesson number two: togetherness.'

Reminds him he'll have to make good on the other night's drunken promise to visit Lou now he's back in town. Maybe this weekend, at the studio in Willesden where he's recording the new album he's calling *Berlin* with Jack Bruce on bass and Aynsley Dunbar on drums. Ideally David would love to poach them both as his own rhythm section on the album he's booked to start next week in France.

'*If I were you, I'd watch my step from now on.*'

But though he knows he can get Aynsley, David can't get Jack. This is good news for Trevor. Since that last hurrah in Hammersmith when he played with a new amp head after some bastards crept in and nicked some of their gear the night before, he's been wise enough to button his lip and, in reward, now gets to pack his bass and passport.

Not so Woody. Before the week is out he'll pick up the phone to hear the voice of Defries sacking him on David's behalf. On the very day he gets married in Sussex.

'*Quite ingenious.*'

And there he'll remain in East Grinstead, in unemployed matrimony surrounded by his new friends in various stages of clarity. Until, in a few months' time, a Sunday newspaper will track him down to ask him about life after David. And Woody will tell them, clear as clear can be, 'I thought a long time before leaving the group, but I believe I made the right decision.'

And that's how he'll choose to remember it.

'*He always did have an inflated opinion of himself.*'

The big bad villain bursts like a balloon. Victory, once again, for our sly English secret agent. Well done, double-O Bowie! Operation Ziggy is complete, the Spiders are dead and David is free. Or is he?

THE END

of

ZIGGY LET DIE

David Bowie will return in

THE MAN WITH THE OILY TONGUE

Ah! The spectre of a new foe.

David's been monitoring him for some time, but now the intelligence is such that he must act and eliminate him.

The name's Ferry – Bryan Ferry, head of Roxy Music. David is a great admirer, though so far their only direct communications have been polite telegrams and bouquets of poinsettias. This is despite having several times been in the same building at the same time, including twice sharing the same bill as David's support last summer. Having yet to break the cagey ice of formal conversation, for now they prefer to signal manoeuvres to one another through the pages of the music press instead. Very carelessly in Bryan's case.

For the past month he's been openly blabbing about his plans for a solo LP comprised of his favourite songs, predominantly from the Sixties. Last week the *Maker* even printed a full provisional tracklisting before he's recorded a note which, when he does, will revolutionise the concept of the covers album for an entire generation. Unless, that is, David can stop him. By beating Bryan to it.

Cue gun barrel, twangy guitar and dripping blood.

Open wide on a tiny village set in miles of flat countryside. Old farmhouses, stone walls, thin winding roads and clumps of lime trees.

On-screen caption: 'Val-d'Oise, France' . . .

IT'S A CHÂTEAU by name, but the reality – especially when the muggy air boils over and down comes the rain in drops the size of slop buckets – feels much less romantic. More a crumbling mansion not 20 miles from the centre of Paris but doing a very successful impression of being the arse end of absolutely nowhere. If not for the wine cellar, the minuscule swimming pool, the tennis court, the ducks, the chickens and the landscape that eventually drove van Gogh to suicide, it's for this rural sense of isolation in a century suspended somewhere between the pages of a Balzac novel that English musicians flock to the studio here at Château d'Herouville.

Marc is no stranger to the ping-pong and billiard room, nor Elton who recommended it to him after discovering it last January when he first came to record the album he named *Honky Château* in its honour. He's been back twice since, the last time just a few weeks ago. Crouch down and press your ear to the flagstones and you might still hear the aftershock of 'Goodbye Yellow Brick Road', like a choral phantom daring any fresh hand to the studio's console to even *try* to build as grand a Notre-Dame.

David won't. Not with this band, a broken Spiders missing their back legs and wincing on their interim crutches: the just-about-indispensable Mick, a twitchy Trevor on bass, an elsewhere Garson on keys and the interloping Aynsley on pots and pans. And not with these songs, borrowed and blue from the Yardbirds, the Pretty Things, the Kinks, the Merseys, the Mojos, the Easybeats, Them, The Who and Syd's Pink Floyd, all recorded with a casual efficiency that does neither the originals nor the careful consideration of Mick's arrangements justice. When he finally puts down his vocals, David oversings, overacts and overeggs, and while the ensuing tribute soufflés don't quite sink, nor do they rise. But then 200 miles away in a studio just above Oxford Circus, Bryan Ferry is adding his own no-less-abominable ululations to what he still thinks is recognisably Elvis Presley's 'Baby I Don't Care'. This race is still anyone's to lose.

In real time the album takes barely a week, but David remains at the Château for three as work and play dissolve into an indistinguishable oneness of cigarettes, headphone levels, sex and vin ordinaire. Late-night trips in a green Cadillac to the discotheques of gayest Paree. Hourless days assembling a strange, long, mood-shifting instrumental, possibly the germ of a whole other album called 'Tragic Moments'. A flying visit from Lulu, who makes husky foreplay out of David's own 'The Man Who Sold The World' and 'Watch That Man' before cackling back to prepare for her Scarborough summer season with Little and Large. Another from Jean from Fanny, whose trysts with David have finally made nudging '*just good friends?*' print and who, because of it, is now a marked woman in Angie's crosshairs.

And the invasion of Twiggy, her manager and photographer fiancé, Justin, and a crew's worth of lights and make-up, including David's own Pierre. They're here to shoot him and Twiggy together for the cover of *Vogue*, which David mistakenly believes will be its first with a male and female couple, not having seen the issue two years ago with actor Alan Bates and model Maudie James on the front.

Justin's only problem with the set-up is that next to Twiggy's Barbados-fresh tan, David's pallor is that of a creature being farmed for veal. Pierre's *magnifique* solution is to draw the outline of masks on their faces: hers lightened to match his alabaster, his a vice versa soft mahogany. David is so pleased with the finished portrait he offers to bypass *Vogue* and license it directly as his new album cover. Justin happily shakes on the deal, flying home with his darling 'Twig' as financially chuffed as he is cruelly unaware that by the time David's record is out she'll have dumped him for the co-star of her latest Hollywood film.

The Château's flagstones hear it all. Every word, every moan, every note, every camera shutter. But David, too lost in warm bodies, white wine and 'Tragic Moments', never hears the flagstones, their phantom whispers beseeching him.

When are you gonna come down? When are you going to land?

WHEN SHE LANDS, the flagstones know. The whole Château knows. Every ear of corn in the surrounding fields quivers to attention. Every tree in the valley straightens. Even the tip of the Eiffel Tower pings like a service bell to the ricochet of her voice 20 miles away.

'DAVID!'

And 'the Bowies' are reunited.

Trailing behind Angie's cases are those of yet another photographer. Because of David's current location and because now 'the Bowies' are the most happening couple of the hour, the *Mirror* wants to shoot them for Paris Fashion Week in a selection of this season's hautest couture. David prefers to stick to his own wardrobe of last season's coolest Fred of the East End, leaving Angie alone to raid the rails of Christian Dior, Ted Lapidus and Loris Azzaro. When the lens cap comes off, David gamely shoves her to the fore. She doesn't protest. Angie hoped this day was coming. It's as they planned it, as they always promised one another, and as he even told a journalist 18 months ago before he'd ever played his first gig as Ziggy.

'We're working on my career first, and then it will be Angie's turn.'

Angie's turn. She is more than ready. But while she feels no shame basking in the spotlight as 'Mrs Bowie' of 'the Bowies', Angie is much too much of her own man to take the lead as someone else's woman.

'I don't believe in trading on the fact you're married to a great talent,' she explains. 'I don't believe in living off him, and at least if you disassociate yourself name wise, you've got a running start.'

So, on your marks, get set, go! As Angie Bowie fades into dust, over the finish line falls all 5 foot 9 inches and 8 stone 3 pounds of . . .

'JIPP JONES!'

Model! Actress! Author of the as-yet-unpublished *The Effects of Intergalactic Visitors on Our Awareness*! Lover of 'tacky junk'! Feminist superheroine who draws greatest satisfaction from 'amusing people or driving them mad!'

And overnight front-page star of Monday's *Daily Mirror*, perching on David's knee in a cocktail dress, head thrown back, laughing like a funfair ball clown. She even gets the headline.

'*Have you met Jipp Jones?*'

But it's a question too far in a country throbbing in the summer heat of too many other urgent hows, whats and whys.

Does *A Clockwork Orange* really breed killers?

Does the Liberal Party really need Rod Stewart's vote?

'*D'you wanna be in my gang?*'

Who raped and strangled two young girls in Sunderland who went out to buy chips and never came back?

Why has Brian Eno quit Roxy Music?

Are Peters and Lee actually married?

Is Keith Chegwin Britain's answer to David Cassidy?

And if Ziggy Stardust is dead, *where* does that leave David Bowie?

NOT IN HADDON HALL. The kids still come, in fewer numbers, but the removal vans have been and gone, the silver ceilings have been repainted, the graffiti scrubbed off the bricks by old Mr Hoy and soon there will be strange and disappointingly unfamous faces opening the door of the ground-floor flat to the sad last stragglers and their drooping felt tips.

So where *is* David Bowie? And *how* can they find him?

'HOW TO MEET YOUR FAVE STAR'

Three cheers for *Mirabelle*! It's not enough that they now have David apparently 'writing' his own weekly column for them, '*My World*', a bit like the one Marc used to have, '*My Scene*'. Or that so do Slade, '*Slade's Crazee Column*', even though Don's not long out of hospital, ribs strapped, leg in a splint, head shaved and stitched and suffering memory lapses so bad he still wakes up not knowing who he is.

No, this week they've surpassed themselves by printing an insider's guide on where girls of 13 best stand a chance of successfully stalking their number 1 pop idol on the streets of London. Starting at hairdresser Ricci Burns in the King's Road where they could catch either of the Jaggers or Suzi Quatro popping in for a trim. Then just down the street to the nearby fashion boutiques: Alkasura, where they might spy Marc or Gary Glitter, or Granny Takes A Trip where Rod Stewart grabs his snazziest gear. Then a spot of lunch at the Hard Rock Cafe on Park Lane where Paul McCartney pops in for the occasional ice cream sundae. And, finally, and assuming the typical pigtails'n'braces *Mirabelle* reader can get past the door, to the Speakeasy club to dance the night away with Keith Moon and David Essex.

Fivepence worth of glorious cotton-headed fantasy, and some of them might even try. But nowhere will they find David Bowie. '*Recording in France,*' the papers keep saying. Then last week it was '*Rome*'. Now this week they say he's '*coming back to Britain*'.

But, in the name of *Jackie* and *Mirabelle*, when?

And in the name of Peters and Lee, *where*?

FOURTEEN

WELCOME HOME. Come on in. And close the door.

It shuts behind him in a mansion flat seesawing between two postcodes, where one kerb starts in Maida Vale and the opposite ends in St John's Wood. The area is recognisably posh, discreetly bohemian, quietly residential but not shy of generating melodrama. The disgraced Lord Lambton used to live round the corner. The photos that ended his political career were taken only yards up the same street in the flat of his prostitute, Norma. And only a few weeks ago there was another to-do with screaming women and ambulances after some mishap at a hippie party when some drunken fool broke his back. A musician from the group Soft Machine. Very lucky to still be alive, now recovering in hospital, though he'll never drum again. And to think it was here where poor Robert Wyatt slipped and fell – from the fourth floor of the block David Bowie now calls home.

Vale Court, W9.

It doesn't feel like home. His new flat is elegantly furnished, but none of it is David's stuff. The paintings, sofas, drawers, bookcases and assorted objets d'art are all the property of its landlords, the actress Diana Rigg and her Israeli artist husband Menachem Gueffen. It wasn't David's choice to rent it, nor Angie's, who'd much prefer somewhere in Chelsea a bit closer to their new pals, the Jaggers. But given the constraints of time – to find somewhere quickly the moment David returned from France – and money – with the funds as restricted by Defries's budget – the pleasantly private if not terribly spacious Vale Court will have to do.

And it does, for now, for David and Angie, and for Zowie and his nanny Daniella, and for Angie's Detroit lover whose own domestic function, much like this month's new ITV sitcom, is that of general man about the house.

But a dark energy lingers on this shady corner of Maida Vale, where musicians plummet near-fatally from windowsills and where the trees flinch to kinky madams whipping their kinkier government ministers. A queer and seedy vibration, infectious and inescapable. And while it may be that what happens to David could have happened to him anywhere – and quite probably would have done – the bald fact remains it happens to him here. Vale Court.

Where *it* starts.

It's been around him oftentimes before, sneaking here and there in afterparties and hotel rooms, in his face and under his nose, just waiting for the chance to fully turn his ignition. So why now?

The Château flagstones know. Because David doesn't want to come down from the fading feeling of being on stage every night. Because much like Sherlock Holmes who took it because he abhorred 'the dull routine of existence', David too 'rebels at stagnation'. Because now he's a number 1 rock star he can afford it. And because the man about the house brings it to his coffee table.

And then it starts.

With a dip of the head and a press of a finger against a nostril. With a sharp sniff, then an upward jerk. With a fidgety pinch of the columella, a watery blink of the eyes and a gurn of the lips. With tingling sinuses, a speeding heart and a nought-to-zillion ego rush that would embarrass Muhammad Ali. With a too-fast-fading euphoria that demands it must begin again. Immediately. Like a young vine creeping along the forest floor that senses a sturdy new trunk, delicately curling around the base before twirling upwards, corkscrewing right to the top until every bough and branch is slowly strangled, so once it starts, it, too, slowly strangles David.

Not his creativity. That – the filthy white crystalline bastard – it perversely assists. Isolates his muse. Sharpens his focus. Compresses his energy. Hardens his resolve. Otherwise he'd want to stop. But it doesn't, and nor does he. And this – *this* – is the real catastrophe.

All it strangles is his humanity. His patience with, his attention to, and his empathy for anyone who isn't David Bowie.

Not straight away. It takes weeks of blowtorching nasal cilia before recreation becomes habit becomes addiction. But it will. Gradually, gram by gram, line by line and sniff by sniff of this monster. This vile poisoned powder. This pollen of impotence posing as rock'n'roll. This bleached soot of slavery fibbing with the empty laugh of freedom. This slimy, teeth-grinding, gum-rubbing, panic-attacking, soul-erasing chalk dust of the living dead.

SNIIIIIIIIIIFF!

It. Has. Started.

EXCESS! Nothing succeeds like it, goes the cliché. But one man's cliché is another's destiny. Some of us are just born to become a disgraced Tory minister. A rock star cokehead. A cigar-chomping bigwig.

The unreadably static face of Tony Defries sucks on the Cuban torpedo in his mouth, stony eyes watching the city stream by through the Cadillac's tinted windows. He is sunk in the back under a cloud of smoke in the cream leather seats he picked out himself, specially perforated to prevent overheating. At the wheel is his chauffeur, Charles. For anyone on the sidewalk stopping to look, which they don't, it's a common enough sight on the streets of Manhattan: a rich cigar-sucking Jew being ferried around town by a black man in a fancy limousine, on his way between the country estate he's just leased in Connecticut to his new office suite on Park Avenue, sixth blocks either way between Saks and Bloomingdale's. There rolls another fat cliché.

Well, why shouldn't he? It is his money.

Mainman's money.

His and David's money.

David's money.

David's money gets David a rented flat in Maida Vale. David's money gets Defries a country pile, Park Avenue and a limo with chauffeur on 24-hour call, not to mention his old Midtown duplex and his new penthouse on the Upper West Side. But that's Mainman economics. It's David's money to make, Defries's money to spend – much of it on building an empire from the outside in. The right Manhattan address. A company car. A fancy new company logo. Extra staff to take messages about taking messages, and return calls about returning calls, and type memos about typing memos, and arrange meetings about arranging meetings in a giddying hustle of bustling industry designed to flabbergast any visitor buzzed into its plant-potted reception. None of whom would for a nanosecond suspect all these people typing, phoning, filing, smiling are just wind-up dummies in an otherwise empty window display. Because take away the people, the desks, the answer machines, the memo pads, the letterheads and the limos, and what *is* 'Mainman'?

One man. David.

Defries's empire is a basket with one egg in it. A big egg, and a very shiny, very golden one at that, but still one egg. Every other to fall into his clutches has either smashed, rolled away or failed to hatch.

He had Iggy, who he dumped, and who because of it has been in freefall ever since, last seen spurting blood from his glass-slashed torso on stage at Max's moments before his good friend, Alice Cooper, rushed him to hospital. He had Mott The Hoople, the only ones ever to dump Defries and who haven't regretted it for a drumbeat: they've just had their first UK hit since shaking off David's Midas touch and will score two more before the year is through. He still has David's friend Dana, still finishing the solo album she started two years ago between Magdalening with Jesus on the West End stage and Mahlering with Ken Russell on a Cumbria film set. And he has Mick, his handsome blond Spider who he coaxed to go solo, soon to return to the Château to start his own album with a little help from David, if only spiritual. And that, as things currently stand in the entire Mainman portfolio of 'talent', is it.

Excepting David himself, that is, already on track to being the biggest-selling albums artist this year with four separate LPs in this week's Top 20. But only in Britain, a land seldom in Defries's Rockefeller daydreams as his Cadillac cruises down Interstate 95, even as the telexes from Mainman's London HQ in Gunter Grove pile up with block-capital panics over unpaid bills and angry creditors. All trivial long-distance dramas, but if they carry on, he might have to shake up his staff over there. Maybe promote that new girl, Corinne? She seems the only cool customer in that office keeping a handle on things right now.

No, it's always been America for Defries. The main goal for Mainman. The only goal. Just frustrating that so far David still hasn't had a Top 10 album here – all that hype and *Aladdin Sane* stalled at 17! – nor a Top 10 single. But that'll change. It will do. It has to, however much money Defries has to throw at it.

And, well, why shouldn't he? It *is* his money.

Mainman's money.

His and David's money.

David's money.

The Cadillac glides on past Central Park like a humidor on wheels. An ocean away in Maida Vale, a fuse is snorted and a brain explodes.

BANG! BANG! BANG! All over London! Bursting out of Embassy fag packets and hollowed-out paperbacks, explosions of yellow tape, gas lighters, torch batteries, wires, wristwatches and Ever Soft Gelemix. Ticking in department stores from Harrods to Liberty's, stuffed inside rolls of fabric, hidden in the pockets of ladies' camel hair coats, men's nylon jackets, suits and dressing gowns, in abandoned Union Jack carrier bags at busy Tube stations, stuffed in wastebaskets outside Marble Arch hotels, in buff quarto-size envelopes waiting in the pigeonholes of the British Legion, the Old Bailey, the Stock Exchange, Number 10 Downing Street and the Bank of England where one inside a book about Shakespeare blows off a man's fingers. Every day, another phone call in an Irish accent, another shop evacuation, another shower of glass, another suspicious package nervously tossed by tongs into a bucket of water. The weather is cooling and the city shivers with fear.

David wipes a nostril and heads to the theatre.

The theatre is actually a prefab cabin in Swiss Cottage, not far from the scene of *Aladdin Sane* and the Holiday Inn Slade fan riot but clinging by enough of an inch of postcode to get away with calling itself Hampstead Theatre Club. The play is a heavy-handed satire about English class that's been panned by reviewers as '*a dead duck*' and '*feebly told*' but it's pulling in the crowds thanks to its casting of the country's most celebrated recovering smack addict.

It's less than a year since Marianne Faithfull was discharged from a treatment hospital in Bexley. Now free from heroin, skin enriched by a holiday in the South Pacific and sporting a smart new androgynous crop by *Mirabelle* stalkers' favourite Ricci Burns on the King's Road, she's bravely making her return to the public eye playing an aristocrat's daughter who dresses like a boy in a Gainsborough painting, doesn't wear a bra and as a rag to a bull is seduced by a lesbian property developer.

David doesn't like *Mad Dog* any more than its withering critics but he likes Marianne, a lot. He's met her before, a long time ago when she was never more famously Marianne Faithfull while he was still namelessly David Jones of the Manish Boys, at different ends of the same Sixties package bill trembling hully-gullys in the knees of teenage Wigan. Nine years later, the footing is a little more even when he visits her dressing room to compliment her performance. Marianne offers him a kiss on the cheek and a glass of wine and he, in turn, offers his ear and a puff of smoke.

'I want to act,' she sighs, eyes misty as a pair of midsummer night dreams. 'And maybe make records again,' she adds coyly. 'They're an easy way to make money.'

David laughs his fangiest laugh. Marianne smiles her pearliest smile. The stars cross, the sun rises, and the city holds its breath for another bomb to blow.

David pinches his septum and heads to another theatre.

The theatre is actually an old cinema on the King's Road, soon to be demolished, but, until then, the second venue to host the show *Gay News* already think '*could well become David Bowie's first movie musical*'. Which is enough of a needle in his competitive eye to book a date with a velvet seat at the Chelsea Classic to see *The Rocky Horror Show* for himself. The papers call it '*witty*', '*camp*', '*exuberant*', '*erotic*', '*wicked*' and '*hilarious*'. David can't really disagree, enjoying it for the rude, schlocky farce as intended, like a more structured and less amateurish *Andy Warhol's Pork*, with tunes. He's also very tickled by lead actor Tim Curry, who as a sweet transvestite from the planet Transsexual spends much of the play in fishnets and corset while bearing an uncanny facial resemblance to David's dear friend Geoff.

It also makes him think. A thought he's had often before in the past, first planted over a decade ago when his 14-year-old bones shook in their theatre seat in awe of Anthony Newley in *Stop the World I Want to Get Off*. A thought now in his head all the time, elbowing for what room it can between the constant starbursts of dopamine.

He sees a stage, the same as Newley's, somewhere in the West End. Himself on it, the same as Newley, not just singing but performing. A plot, the same as Newley's, played out with a supporting cast. His name, the same as Newley's, up in lights on the same marquee, for months, for weeks, the hottest ticket in town. Greasepaint! Footlights! 'Break a leg'! Curtain calls! Bouquets flung from the loggia boxes!

Oh, no. David? Surely *Gay News* were only *joking*? That is, you don't *actually* mean . . . your own *musical*?

THE HILLS ARE ALIVE with the sound of school bells. Ringing like the jangle of so many keys in so many jail doors. The lucky kids to have survived the summer of '73 without being raped and bludgeoned on the way to the chip shop, or murdered walking home from the disco, or electrocuted after dragging a Dansette too close to the bath, or burned alive in the Summerland amusement park fire on the Isle of Man, or blown to bits by a bomb in a carrier bag trudge back to their desks to the galley-slave number 1 rhythm of Donny Osmond's 'Young Love'. New shoes not yet scuffed, new blazers with dangling orangutan sleeves not yet snotted, new trousers not yet caned, new pens not yet spreading gossip on cubicle walls, new pigtails not yet pulled, new skirts not yet hitched, new PE kits not yet soaked in cross-country blizzards, new lunch money not yet spent on fags not yet puffed behind bike sheds, new haircuts upon heads not yet sent home with disapproving notes to parents. But they will be.

In assembly halls north, south, east and west, spluttering headmasters gawp, unable to believe their own mothball eyes.

A 16-year-old Welsh girl swanning into Cynffig Comprehensive with green highlights in her natural auburn curls!

A 14-year-old boy from Derby slouching into Shelton Lock Secondary with a head of flaming pillar-box red!

A bright girl of 15 from Bournemouth buzzing into Summerbee Secondary with hair streaked vivid blue and yellow!

Just what, or *who*, is responsible for this epidemic of anarchy?

'David Bowie,' says Julie in Wales.

'David Bowie,' says Andy in Derby.

'David Bowie,' says Valerie in Bournemouth. She paid £4 for her blue Ziggy cut-and-dye and isn't washing it out anytime soon. 'David is my idol,' she protests. 'And nearly everyone says they like my hair – even some of the teachers. I love school and I don't want to leave, but I think this is very unfair.' So do her classmates. Eight boys rush to the barber asking for a spiky-on-top 'Bowie cut' in solidarity. Another girl of 13 pledges Bowie rebel allegiance by bleaching her fringe: she, too, is suspended. '*Quite right,*' the *Daily Mail* applaud. '*Why should teachers relax the tyranny of gymslip and blazer to make way for the sartorial dictatorship of a mincing pop idol with camped-up coiffure?*'

And so the tyranny stands firm. As the Education Secretary Mrs Thatcher would doubtless remind them, since children should only be seen and not heard, those who try a little *too* hard to be seen should be erased altogether like bad sums off a blackboard. And if school doesn't do it, the outside world will. Because this time next week there'll be two more dead 16-year-old girls strangled walking home through the woods after a disco in Swansea. And come Monday morning, the same bells will still be ringing and the same playgrounds will still be singing.

Gonna be alright, dancin' on a Saturday night . . .

FIFTEEN

A DULL WARM DAY in September and the clocks are striking nine thirty. A thick crowd mills on Kensington High Street, heaving towards the five-storey concrete, iron and glass art deco temple, once the department store Derry & Toms but as of this morning the Ministry of Dreams. On the stroke of half past the doors swing open, and with the first foot over the threshold the reveries begin.

Of suddenly being zapped centre stage into a glitzy Hollywood musical. Any minute now, surely, Fred Astaire will come tap-tap-tapping across the cream marble flooring, heel and toe like castanets, hand outstretched ready to clasp Ginger whose every twirl will be multiplied a hundred times over in the vast surrounding kaleidoscope of mirrors. And round they'll spin, past potted ferns and ostrich feathers, court shoes and mock ocelot handbags, tobacco lipsticks and rose chokers, through the florist, the bookshop and the exotic Casbah market, dancing all the way down the stairs to the basement food hall where reveries become even wilder hallucinations.

Tins of baked beans stacked in a giant replica Heinz tin. Sardines in a giant sardine tin with rolled-back lid. Tinned meats in a giant ham tin. Soups in a giant Warhol Campbell's soup tin. Bread from a giant bread bin. Tea from a giant tea caddy. Pet food from the belly of a giant Great Dane. Soap powder from a giant soap packet. Fish from a giant fishing boat. Wine in a mock wine cellar and a tiled dairy complete with painted pigeon droppings.

Waltzing back up to the first floor, more mirrors and chocolate-brown carpet, giraffe-print coats and fake Persian lamb jackets hanging from hat stands, there to be tried on in changing rooms looking like doorways to Cleopatra's palace, their walls decked with tiger and leopard skin.

Skipping to the second floor, a children's Disneyland with fairy-tale castle, Wild West saloon, a carousel of toys, oversized Snoopy kennel, shelves shaped like Peter Rabbit, a kids' roundabout shaped like a record player, a sweet bar and soda shop with magic toadstool tables, a maternity zone with similarly ginormous wardrobes and chairs to make their swollen-bellied mothers feel less hideously obese, and a New Orleans-style boutique for girls aged between 9 and 13 unnervingly named 'Lolita's'.

Hotstepping on, up to the third, and its ginger carpets, black counters and walls of yellow ochre, where men are men who want satin gowns, canes and monocles and, most of all, to place their money where their ego is in the special boudoir section named 'Mistresses': frighteningly expensive jewelled bras and matching G-string sets, others in space age silver, all awaiting aroused rub and sweating purchase, laid out on display on a circular bed of yet more leopard skin.

Fandangoing through the fourth floor: brown marble and home furnishings, china dinner sets, luminous brooms, lurex brocade cushions, kitsch prints by Tretchikoff and rattan furniture.

High-kicking up to the grand finale of the fifth. The proverbial top hat of the Rainbow Room restaurant. Its ceiling, an illuminated colour spectrum. Its floor, apricot marble. Its tables, decorated with peach tablecloths and black orchids. Its lamps, bronze female nude statuettes. Its bar, peach glass. Its ambience, the idle-rich tinkle of a white Cunard Line piano. A dining room weighing heavy on Jay Gatsby's side of paradise, and, if the press are correct that thanks to the imminent Fitzgerald film adaptation starring Robert Redford jazz-age decadence is the hottest new fashion, then the Rainbow Room is its scorching height. Up here, grey dangerous 1973 feels a lot further than an elevator ride away. But like everything else in this out-of-body shopping experience that inhales Harrods and exhales Ken Russell, it's supposed to. That's why Big Biba cost a devilish £666,000 to create.

The first morning of trade in Barbara Hulanicki's imperial new premises, apart from one French shoplifter caught trying to steal a £6 hat and a 33p pack of playing cards, all is as smooth as the waxed marble floors. Women who came only to look and touch leave mystified to be suddenly laden with carrier bags swinging with black-and-gold tins of Biba baked beans, Biba lime skin freshener, gold bangles, sparkly wellies and spotted eye-veiled hats they had no idea they needed an hour ago. Wandering home, happy and dazed, back out to a cold colourless Seventies reality as insipid as a 40-calorie slice of Nimble bread.

Where pain and misery are only a train timetable away.

Half past midday, and as the first lunches of boiled beef and fish stew are served in the Rainbow Room, across town in King's Cross station a baby-faced youth in a blue V-neck sweater tosses a package into a disused booking hall by platform 8 then runs for dear life. Seconds later, it's raining glass in a gale of screams.

Twenty-three minutes past one, bang goes another down the road in Euston, injuring seven. By mid-afternoon, Waterloo and Charing Cross are next to be shut down after more telephoned warnings of hidden devices about to blow. So has Victoria, where last Saturday five more were hospitalised by a bomb in a Woolworths bag.

How long before the next one's a Biba bag?

'*In every dream home . . .*'

As the Euston brooms sweep up the debris and the Kensington tills gobble up the pounds, an eerie record spins in Vale Court.

David has played it many times since he bought it in May, sticking true to his vow to a reporter that, having travelled round the world, one of the first things he intended to do once he returned to England was 'buy the new Roxy Music album'. That first listen back in Haddon Hall was with an awe and intrigue skewered by the strong and savage heart-thumping dread of a sweaty-browed gambler in a high-stakes poker game at the moment they ask the villain to show their hand. In his, 'Aladdin Sane' and 'Time'. In theirs, 'For Your Pleasure' and 'The Bogus Man'. The pot is split.

'*. . . a heartache.*'

Still, poor Bryan. All those months planning his new covers album, *These Foolish Things*, only for David to come along and schedule his, called *Pin Ups*, for release on the very same day. Or perhaps not so poor Bryan. After all, his is still the gizzard captivating David's stylus as he sits back, cigarette sucking, nostrils zinging while a woman's fingers softly tap his thigh in time to Roxy's rumbling baroque.

The fingers aren't Angie's. She's currently in America, leaving him here with his man about the house to gallivant after Mick Jagger backstage with the Stones at Wembley, and anything and anyone else he fancies. So much the better if Jagger used to fancy them too.

'Darling,' laughs Marianne, as only Marianne can. 'Of *course* I know her!'

The smoke of their cigarettes mingles in a wispy kiss above the black record sleeve on Marianne's lap. It shows a tall sultry blonde in a strapless black leather dress. She wears matching opera gloves, stiletto heels and a pillbox hat, one hand on her hip, the other outstretched walking a panther on a leash. The sum total is like a pervy Pirelli calendar version of Rita Hayworth in *Gilda*. On the inner gatefold credits she is listed as simply 'Amanda'.

'That's *my* Amanda, darling. Amanda Lear.'

Marianne knows her from modelling together – they've both catwalked at fashion shows for their friend, and David's, Ossie Clark, which is where Bryan first approached her to be the cover star of Roxy's *For Your Pleasure*.

'She knows Dalí. Oh, Dalí simply *adores* her!'

As a 12-inch square image of leatherette lust, so does David.

'Shall I call her?' asks Marianne, stretching to the telephone without waiting for his answer. She dials, smiling mischievously, abstractedly rubbing the pearls round her neck as the tones ring.

'Amanda? Darling, it's Marianne! Listen, I'm sitting here beside a fan of yours. He's simply *dying* to meet you. I'm passing over the phone now. Be kind to him.'

She slips the receiver to David. He shows no sign of nerves as he presses it to his ear.

'Hello. Amanda? I'm David Bowie.' *Sniff*. 'I'd like to meet you . . .'

MARIANNE IS STILL THERE to greet her at the door. 'Be cool, darling,' she whispers. 'He's crazy about you. He'll be putty in your hands.'

A thick overture of Jungle Gardenia perfume sweeping up David's nose prepares him for her entrance. Nothing quite prepares him for her presence.

Skinny as a javelin, lifelike as a mannequin, hair of tumbling gold, lips of glossy ruby with cheekbones that could slice the rind off a rasher of bacon in a single stroke. Her mouth opens and out tumbles 'hallooo' in the accent of a Russian spy trying to pass as Miss France: a Rosa Klebb trapped in the body of a Barbie doll. If Amanda isn't a woman, then she's the most beautiful drag queen he's seen in his life. And, of course, Marianne is right. Putty in her hands.

Left alone in the back seat of a limousine, his putty fingers clasp hers and refuse to let go. It is very late as they drive through town towards his suggested dinner date, Tramp, the elite members-only club and restaurant discreetly tucked round the back of Fortnum & Mason. 'The only place that will serve food this time of night,' David assures her before gently steering the conversation to Dalí.

'Would you say he's a genius?'

Amanda has not long recovered from a dose of flu. Looking her suitor up and down as the streetlights dapple through the windows, from his skinny green trousers up to his face white with ivory foundation, his goblin's teeth, his shaved eyebrows and russet bangs poking out from under a green cap, talking eagerly about surrealism between a morse code of constant sniffs and cigarette puffs, a part of her wonders if this isn't all some feverish bad dream. Then he squeezes her hand, warm and strong. No. This is real, alright.

Real as the faces of the Jaggers, Mick and Bianca, sat in one of the table booths where Amanda is led after stepping down into a wood-panelled basement with wall-mounted candelabras and chandeliers, bathed in red and blue light. The vicious rumour is that in a pre-electric age Tramp used to be the scene of aristocratic debauchery between kings and their mistresses, something neither the regency décor nor today's clientele, whether arms dripping with one type of sparkle or noses with another, make much effort to dispel.

Amanda and Mick needn't be introduced, but David does, unaware that as an ex-lover of Mick's dead friend Brian Jones he's already clocked and indexed her as one of the more stubborn lingering stains of the Sixties before she pulls up a chair. Bianca, another mutual friend of Ossie Clark if otherwise a stranger, greets her with the same look she'd just about spare on the laying down before her of a waiter's fresh bread basket. David, much too eager to resume the conversation as he left it with Mick three nights ago backstage at Wembley, pays no attention, lights another cigarette, orders some wine and gently strokes Amanda's leg under the table while directing her to the menu card. Parma ham and melon, baby poussin, grilled sole, bangers and mash and 12 different types of burger, one for every sign of the zodiac. The boys, Capricorn and Leo, gas on about music. The girls, Scorpio and Taurus, play with their lettuce and French fries.

'Right,' announces Mick once the plates are cleared. 'Let's see this fight.'

It is nearly 2 a.m. in London, and even the Provo who this afternoon will plant a bomb in an Oxford Street menswear shop is fast asleep in his bed. But the vampire hours of rock'n'roll have not quite finished their shift.

'The fight' Mick speaks of is a heavyweight revenge match between Muhammad Ali and the ex-Marine who broke his jaw in the ring six months ago, Ken Norton. Although it's taking place eight time zones away at the Forum in Los Angeles it's also being screened live on closed-circuit TV at cinemas around the world, including the Odeon in Leicester Square, a short totter from Tramp where Mick leads them, tickets at the ready, braced for 12 rounds of slugging black muscle.

David leans in close to Amanda's ear. 'Our first date,' he whispers, practically kissing it, 'and we're going to the cinema just like young lovers.'

But no kissing in the back row once the bell rings. Round one and all 212 pounds of Ali is up on his toes dancing. All 205 of Norton lunges, misses and swings at empty rope. The ringside commentators are breathless. David's hand glides along Amanda's skirted thigh.

'*The first round is over! Muhammad Ali did everything he said he would!*'

Round two, and Norton is met with the war dance of the Ali shuffle. A left jab backs Ali into the corner. Norton picks him up and sets him down on the ropes like a naughty child. Both men perspire profusely. David and Amanda's fingers interlock.

'That's a sweet jab he's got going!'

Round three, a good left–right combination from Norton, then a right upper cut by Ali.

'They better be in condition, cos they're movin'!'

David leans across, tapping Mick on the knee, makes his excuses and, clutching Amanda's hand, leads her back out into the last dawn-daring dribble of Piccadilly night.

The taxi drops them off at her place in Chelsea, a large studio apartment walled with art deco prints. He immediately recognises them.

'Erté? I collect him too.'

'They're not mine,' she says, stifling a yawn. 'This flat isn't mine. I'm just looking after it for my friend, Susannah. Sorry, but it is very late and I'm very tired.'

'That's OK.' *Sniff.* 'You don't mind if I stay . . . do you?'

The bedroom is downstairs. What last lingering doubts David may still have about Amanda's gender are removed there by morning. And though she never tells him, because there's no need, how much more pleasure might he have gained knowing the very bed in which he satisfies his enquiry was dragged up the stairs and into the apartment on the day she moved in by a very good friend of hers. Bryan Ferry.

SIXTEEN

AUTUMN COMES in oranges and yellows and flutes and flugelhorns. As the leaves curl and fall in Maida Vale, the tune vibrating the lips of the men carrying David and Angie's boxed possessions out of Vale Court and into the back of a van is a gentle jig.

'*Da dee-dee-dee . . .*'

They're still humming it as they wait at the traffic lights on Edgware Road, bound south.

'. . . *Dada dee-dee-dee-dee . . .*'

Round Hyde Park and the back of Buck House.

'. . . *Dadada dee . . .*'

Cutting through Belgravia, west onto the King's Road.

'. . . *Dada, dee dee deeee.*'

Turning left just past Chelsea Town Hall, pulling up at the kerb about halfway down a terrace of tall thin Queen Anne houses. Number 89 Oakley Street.

'*Pom, pom-pom-pom.*'

Arms full of packing cases, art nouveau standard lamps and wardrobe trunks, they carry on up the stone steps and into the narrow hallway, still pom-ing and da-ing and dee-ing. They, and everybody else. Milkmen and posties, policemen and traffic wardens, window cleaners and road sweepers, butchers and grocers, porters and doormen, dinner ladies and checkout girls. All sufferers of the same deadly melodic plague that's turned the entire country into one giant human kazoo, first germinating between the ears of a Dutchman as a piece of library music given the title 'Eye Level'. For the past year it's been incubating as the theme to an ITV series about an Amsterdam police detective, just back on air for its second season on Wednesday nights straight after *Man About the House*. This is its moment of contagion. By the third episode, the orchestra recording conducted by a 27-year-old Englishman, Simon Park, is shifting over 50,000 copies a day. By the fourth, it's outselling Wizzard's sickly 'Angel Fingers', The Sweet's *Rocky Horror*-ish 'Ballroom Blitz' and the latest vulture on glam's carcass, David Essex, now cashing in on his *That'll Be the Day* screen fame with some half-chewed Fifties nostalgia over a funky rip-off of Ringo's 'Back Off Boogaloo' called 'Rock On'. None of whom have the faintest idea why it isn't them at number 1 but the jolly oompah of *Van der Valk*.

It's still there the week David and Angie, minus the departed man about the house, move into their new rented Chelsea townhouse. Angie, of course, was the one who found it, and after much cajoling Defries generously agreed to pay the £600-a-month rent. Out of David's money.

Possibly Angie would have thought twice about the location had she known her new bedroom windows looked directly across to the rear of the flat on Glebe Place where her husband's been regularly inspecting etchings with Amanda. And where, in terms of pavement inches, he can now pop over at a convenience even closer than that between Lord Lambton and Norma. But Angie doesn't know, not yet. The same way Amanda still doesn't know David's married.

In every other respect Oakley Street is the perfect spot. Tucked between the Embankment and the King's Road, less than a mile from Mainman's now all but neglected London office on Gunter Grove, less than a quarter from the Jaggers' house facing the river on Cheyne Walk, only a few minutes through light traffic to the door of Tramp and an even shorter limo ride to their favourite nightspots in Kensington and the Fulham Road. Among them Laurita's, London's first 'soul food' restaurant and jazz club serving fried chicken, black-eyed peas, sweet potato pie and peach cobbler, swathed in red velvet and peacock feathers and named after its larger-than-life host, a black clairvoyant from New York and

Angie's new best friend. As fate would have it, Laurita lives round the corner from Oakley Street on the same road as Amanda, Glebe Place. Which David will find very handy when he starts sleeping with her too.

Does he care? Does he count them? Does *anyone*?

Well, now, let's see. So there's Angie, technically, and there's Marianne, and there's still Jean from Fanny when she's in town, and there's Amanda, and there's Laurita. That's already a whole handful. Moving on, then, sixth finger.

Ava.

She finds him like a heat-seeking missile. All the way from New York where they first clicked back in February, over to France where she just misses him at the Château, finally turning up in London with her cropped bleached hair and her shiny salivating eyes and her reminder to make good on his Gramercy Park sweet nothings about hiring her as a backing singer. Which he does, in the same breath asking her to move in with him and Angie at Oakley Street. Which she does, taking occupancy of the top guest room.

There are five floors, including the self-contained basement flat where Freddie and Daniella move in: he as a one-man Biba designing and fitting clothes for David and Angie to order, she as general helper and Zowie's nanny. Above it, the ground-floor kitchen and dining room with pine table and chairs and blue floral Chinese carpet. On the first floor, a split lounge: one half the music room cluttered with pianos, guitars, Moogs, saxophones and various pieces of recording equipment; the other, a white shagpile-carpet living room with fibreglass ball chairs and central sunken white leather pit scattered with blue and silver cushions for flopping and watching either the giant TV or his 16mm film projector, the surrounding walls decorated with modern airbrushed pop art and framed photos of James Dean stockpiled from the King's Road rock'n'roll boutique that was called Let It Rock, now Too Fast To Live, Too Young To Die. On the second floor is Zowie's bedroom, next door to David and Angie's with its sunken satin king-size bed, a walk-in wardrobe, another giant TV and some of their favourite art nouveau pieces from Haddon Hall, including a Daum bowl and a Gallé vase. Lastly, the top office, and beside it the guest room. For now, Ava's room.

She's not there long. Angie can deal with David's concubines but not when she has to see the same face every day helping themselves to her orange juice. Once David receives the permission of Defries to spend his own money bankrolling another mistress – just as he's done with Amanda, now on Mainman's books to pay for the singing lessons she needs to become a pop star – Ava moves into her own apartment on the King's Road. About the same distance round one corner from Oakley Street as Amanda's and Laurita's round the other. Like Lord Lambton said, 'Sometimes people like variety.'

And doesn't he look one himself, Lord Bowie of his new Chelsea manor, literally encircled by courtesans, all barely a finger's snap away. Sat there, smiling, smoking, sipping, snorting in his South West 3 paradise, wondering what to do, who to ring, where to go, who to fuck. Hilarious, really. No wonder he sits there laughing.

'*HA! HA! HA!*'

But not for very long.

THE LITTLE SHIT. It creeps up on David when he least expects, when his head is fizzing with so many plans that each week in every pop paper scoop after Bowie scoop cancels out the other.

SCOOP! His West End musical, '*a legitimate Broadway style revue*' with the working title '*1984*', believed to be '*a musical adaptation of George Orwell's famous novel of the same name which predicted a Britain of the future under the iron rule of the tyrant Big Brother*'. Providing Defries can sort the rights with Orwell's widow, it should be touring the provinces next March before settling in London at the Prince of Wales Theatre where David '*will definitely be playing the lead role of Winston Smith*'.

SCOOP! In tandem, conflicting stories that David's musical will '*open on Broadway*' and resurrect '*the story of Ziggy Stardust*'. But whichever he decides, it'll definitely be some sort of collaboration with New York experimental theatre director Tony Ingrassia who David first met two years ago when he brought *Andy Warhol's Pork* to London.

SCOOP! And there's his Sixties covers album *Pin Ups*, like its predecessor already certified gold on pre-orders, and its lead single, a smooth version of the Merseys' 'Sorrow' in the shops any day now.

Which is when the little shit turns up.

'*HA! HA! HA!*'

Literally laughing at David in the Top 10.

'*HEE! HEE! HEE!*'

The godawful worst of it being that it *is* David in the Top 10.

A different David. A younger David. But still David.

A David not long turned 20 in April 1967 – when the Summer of Love was ripening ready to bloom, when Number 10 still stank of Wilson's pipe smoke, when Steed and Mrs Peel had just gone Technicolor, when the Sinatras were at number 1 with 'Somethin' Stupid' and Manfred Mann not far behind with 'Ha! Ha! Said The Clown', and when David's even stupider '*HA! HA! HA!*' released that month sank without trace. And thank Christ it did, if only to spare him the fate of becoming a Sixties novelty one-hit-wonder.

'You know? That gnome bloke.'

But now it's back. The little shit. Cackling in his face like cool-sucking antimatter to everything he's achieved these past 18 months.

'And now the new one from David Bowie – "The Laughing Gnome"!'

Decca. The bastards. Six years ago they first put it out on their Deram imprint. But even though it flopped, they never actually deleted it. Which means no one, not even a furious Defries, can stop them repressing and repromoting it.

At least his critics know cynical opportunism when they hear it.

'*Deram have lumbered jolly David with this re-release of a 1967 piece of absolute garbage,*' howls the *NME*.

'*It would serve Decca right if Bowie fans saw this enterprise for what it really is,*' agrees *Disc*.

But the public don't. Not this public, flailing in the post-glam apocalypse of reason where even a new single by Slade can't outsell the assembled tooting oboes of *Van der Valk*. A public who not so long ago punted The Goons' barmy old 'Ying Tong Song' into the Top 10 for a laugh, just as they've done this month with Bobby 'Boris' Pickett and the Crypt-Kickers' schlock Sixties novelty 'Monster Mash'. A public who take to the 'Ying Tong' battiness and 'Eye Level' catchiness of 'The Laughing Gnome' like class clowns to a whoopee cushion.

So up the little shit climbs, up, up, up into the Top 10 until the producers of *Top of the Pops* are faced with something of a dilemma. Any other week, and they'd probably get Pan's People to choreograph a dance routine, doubtless dressed in curly shoes and caps with bells on, jiving round giant papier-mâché toadstools. But the week it jumps to number 8, the girls are busy stretching their leotards to an Isley Brothers disc instead. And so the BBC have to resort to their standard Plan B. Make their own comedy promo film, just as they did with 'Monster Mash'.

And – '*HA! HA! HA!*' – just in time for the programme's historic 500th episode too! A specially extended one-hour extravaganza including filmed birthday messages from Slade and Mick Jagger, where Bryan Ferry sneers and tics through his camp new Dylan cover, where The Who wreck a drumkit, where David Cassidy serenades a Pan Am jumbo jet, and where a ludicrous orange-haired Bowie lookalike is chased down the street by a garden gnome. Watched by millions.

'*HEE! HEE! HEE!*'

In Chelsea, David sniffs and turns another page of Orwell.

'*People were leaping up and down in their places and shouting at the tops of their voices in an effort to drown the maddening bleating voice that came from the screen.*'

He isn't laughing.

SEVENTEEN

HE'D HAVE ASKED PIERRE to do his face, but he's busy in Belgium doing Jagger's on tour with the Stones. David's fault for recommending him to Mick in the first place. So instead he's got the very English and equally capable Barbara Daly, the cosmetics queen famous for creating the droog make-up in *A Clockwork Orange*. Her colours blended and his lips glossed, the cameras roll.

He's on a small chequerboard stage dressed toe to tie in white, surrounded by dancers in cobweb leotards. At one end is a piece of low scaffolding where a very shiny and very glamorous Amanda perches in a black collared cape wielding a giant pole wrapped with Christmas tinsel. Every now and then she pokes one of the dancers with it as David shuffles at a snail's pace singing 'Sorrow'. He's supposed to be the White Knight, she the Black Queen and the dancers the remaining chess pieces in a homage to *Alice in Wonderland*, which anyone willing to stretch their imagination far beyond the limits of harshly lit videotape is welcome to try. Once the song fades Amanda has a few lines of spoken dialogue. She says them in her very best English, which to anyone who actually speaks it sounds like English yet to be descrambled by some Soviet variant of the Enigma machine. David looks up at her and smiles a patient persevering smile. It's going to be a long three days.

Day one. A Thursday in the Marquee on Wardour Street, the chosen location to shoot David's first American network TV special to air next month on NBC. It's one of three episodes of their late Friday night music showcase *The Midnight Special* filming in London this month, a major coup for Defries in his otherwise uphill struggle to break David in America. But as the 'Sorrow' scene demonstrates it's very cramped, very makeshift and very tight on budget. The official line is they're in the Marquee because it ties in with the Sixties R&B roots of his new *Pin Ups* album. The truth is, it's all they could afford and far too small: once you've wheeled in two bulky TV cameras there's barely room to swing a tinselled scaffolding pole. This first night is only a little easier as there's no live audience yet, just the crew, the dancers, David, Amanda and Marianne, who David's coaxed to resume the singing career she abandoned several hundred prescriptions ago. Commencing tonight, on the same chequerboard set, with Noël Coward's 'Twentieth Century Blues' sung in a whispering moan that couldn't grip the melody any limper had she attempted it under general anaesthetic.

Day two, Friday, and a small audience trickles in, the first to see David perform anywhere in public since Hammersmith. But only after more Marianne, looking gorgeous in a chiffon and pearly satin gown if no less puny of pipes, that voice forever stuck on the blow-football subs bench cunningly disguised by lip-synching to her original 1965 hit version of 'As Tears Go By'. Then, at last, David, not quite miming but singing to a backing track of 'Time', frolicking in a blue flame-patterned leotard, swirling his wrists in camp protest against the producers' insistence he enunciate 'wanking' as 'swanking'. The crowd whoop and cheer, make-believing it's a proper gig. But even they know it's still only a warm-up.

Day three, Saturday. This is The Big Day.

The youngest ones are out their front door and on their way even before the *Hair Bear Bunch!* By the time *Joe 90* has finished some of them are already here, bracing the Saturday morning drizzle of a cold neon Soho, a nervous serpent of best clothes and bright make-up slinking down the east side of Wardour Street. The pink tickets most of them won in a free fan club lottery, apart from the eight given away by *The Sun*, told them to be here for 11, round about when *The Partridge Family* starts. As it is, the queue doesn't really get moving until well into *Tarzan* with Ron Ely after half past, and it's only by *World of Sport* that all 200 are safely inside the Marquee where Saturday daytime becomes a night all the darker for its newly repainted black walls. It will be hours before any of them breathe fresh air again. None of them care. These few hundred kids know they're the envy of every frantic plea in this week's classifieds: '*BOWIE TV show ticket wanted, exorbitant price.*' Because unlike last night, *they're* the ones who are actually going to see him *live* with a *band* for the first time since the Spiders.

If not, alas, *the* Spiders. Instead, the same core *Pin Ups* ensemble of Mick on guitar, Trevor on bass, Aynsley on drums and Garson on piano. They've been rehearsing for the past week in a space above Selmer music shop on Charing Cross Road with the extra rhythm guitar of David's young Haddon Hall neighbour Mark: the one who used to be in the Arnold Corns, the one who loaned him his Les Paul for the *Ziggy* LP cover and the one who David will introduce on stage at the Marquee for reasons best known to himself as 'Mark Two Rivers, a Mohican from Penge'. There's also a small brass section and a trio of backing singers who David names 'The Astronettes', resurrecting that of Lindsay Kemp's dance troupe at his Rainbow shows last summer. They include his good friend Geoff, also on congas, a leather clothes designer and friend of Laurita's named Jason, and Ava. Meaning between her, Amanda and Marianne, David will be sharing his TV special with at least three current bedfellows.

And with two other bands he's also invited. One old, the Troggs, who only last Christmas the *NME* were asking '*Was this the first punk rock band?*' And one new, Carmen, chosen as a goodwill gesture to his rekindling friendship with their producer Tony Visconti, who look a bit like a prog-rock *High Chaparral* and, sure enough, sound a bit like Curved Air gone flamenco. Along with Marianne and Amanda – here under David's suggested pseudonym 'Dooshenka', as in the Russian for 'darling' – this is his assembled cast for the *Midnight Special* episode he subtitles *The 1980 Floor Show*. Somewhere between a promo for *Pin Ups*, a fan farewell to Ziggy and a foreshadow of his *1984* musical that's already looking increasingly sketchy in terms of any consent from Orwell's estate. 'Actually, we still don't have the rights,' Ingrassia only now admits. 'So it's possible we may have to call it *1983* or something like that.'

Ingrassia is also here at the Marquee, stressing over his choice of Eighties as he loiters by the bar with the rest of Saturday's VIPs, including several of his old friends from *Andy Warhol's Pork*. There's Cherry, now

Mainman publicist and ghostwriter of David's new *Mirabelle* column, and Leee, latter Iggy pool lifeguard and Mainman's 'vice president'. And another old *Pork*er, in full make-up, a blonde wig, a stuffed bra, a short red negligée, fishnet stockings, suspenders, heels and red gloves clutching a metal handbag inscribed 'Campus Queen': rattling inside, a pair of handcuffs.

Wayne County is back in town.

In town and grabbing his tits on the front page of *Melody Maker*.

'*WAYNE COUNTY, New York's latest rock outrage has been signed to Tony Defries's Mainman company which also manages David Bowie.*'

He's been flown over to meet the London press by Defries, also here with a cigar sticking from his face like a sherbet fountain. Though exactly *why* anyone who couldn't manage Iggy would take on a singer who usually dresses like a cross between Tammy Wynette and a Nazi stormtrooper, has the name of his favourite band The Dave Clark Five stuck in his wig, is known to eat dog food out of a toilet pan and who for a set climax likes to take an actual shit on stage is something of a mystery.

But today Wayne is on best behaviour, propping up the bar, flashing his handcuffs, squawking like a one-man *Whatever Happened to Baby Jane?* and keeping the reporters entertained while they and the kids grin and bear Carmen. Every one of them wondering how much more bolero histrionics they can take before David shows his face.

IT FINALLY APPEARS AT 3 O'CLOCK. White as a fridge, grinning like a ventriloquist's dummy, diamante earring swinging. 'Hello,' it says. 'So, what have you been up to?' And the shrieking begins.

For a small stage there are an awful lot of people on it: David, in a loose satin top and yellow slacks; the five members of his band, all in black except Mick in luminescent white; the three Astronettes up front – Geoff and Jason in tie-front open shirts, Ava in a red skirt, stripey halter top and Biba giraffe-print hat; and the three-man brass section, all in white rollnecks, hanging off in the wings.

It looks every bit as cluttered as it sounds. The first stab at the first *Pin Ups* number, 'Everything's Alright', falls apart before the last chorus. David sighs and smiles down at the kids in the front row, still quivering in

Bowie-eyed shellshock, all flapping pens, LPs and autograph books under his nose, bleating his name over and over in disbelief.

'Frustrating innit!' he grins.

Drumsticks click, and the song starts again. This time everything nearly is alright. David laughs. 'I'm out of condition!'

A man wearing a headset behind one of the giant cameras signals him. 'Again?' winces David.

Again.

So begins a long day's journey into a night of endless déjà vu. This isn't a gig at all. This is television production at its most tortuously monotonous. Take after take after take until the producers are satisfied, and the second they are, David immediately slips off for a lengthy costume change. In total he and his band perform just six songs today: it takes them seven hours.

He first returns as a fully regurgitated Ziggy, in the same stripey suit he wore on his last tour, for 'Space Oddity'. Then lace-up thigh-high stiletto boots and a black feathery red PVC bodice for another *Pin Ups* cover, The Who's 'I Can't Explain'. Next a black cobweb top and gold leotard ensemble, with two glittery mannequin hands sewed on his breast so it looks like he's being grabbed from behind. There was a saucy third hand grabbing his crotch which the producers asked him to remove on grounds of taste. Unwisely, as they realise the moment he launches into 'The Jean Genie' and his newly exposed Lycra groin bobs and thrashes like a raccoon in a binbag.

'We've written a musical,' says David, now in his old Space Samurai suit. 'And this is the title song, "1984".'

It's the first time anyone's heard his funky new Orwell overture. It starts a bit like the Temptations' 'Papa Was A Rolling Stone', then segues into a medley with another upbeat soul tune about the book's sinister Junior Spies, currently titled 'You Didn't Hear It From Me', a cue for David to have his covers ripped off, exposing a semi-topless costume with a large keyhole motif. But like every other song played today, it's a stop-start mess. There are problems with the tempo, the band not quite catching its 'Shaft'-like groove, and with Mick, whose tuning has been queasy all day in the intense heat of the TV lights. Normally, on stage he rarely breaks a string, but here they're snapping like a stripper's garter belt.

Just when they've nearly nailed '1984', another one kapoings. So does David's patience. He stomps off.

He stomps back on for the last time just before 9.45 p.m., arm in arm with Marianne. She wears a rectangular nun's wimple and a long black shroud covering her whole body. The shroud has slits up each side loose enough to flap open, which it does. And it's then, when it does, which it does often, that everyone, including Angie watching from the bar bouncing Zowie in her arms, can plainly see Marianne's naked bottom. Front and back.

Beside her, David, once more in his feathery red PVC and hooker boots, waits for the weedy flutes to count them into a duet of Sonny & Cher's 'I Got You Babe'. When they come, David sings it like David. Marianne like a dying battery. As a fat cherry on the cake, it's as sour as the shambles of *The 1980 Floor Show* deserves.

If they want to, the kids can hang around after David and watch the Troggs. It's gone 10 p.m. None of them want to. If they're lucky, some might be home for the end of *Parkinson* by the second take of 'Wild Thing', witnessed only by the last stragglers at the bar. The hardier hard-drinking journalists, some of David's crew and Trevor, looking over at the stage where he's just been standing, a beer in his hand and a sad smile on his face as Reg Presley makes his heart sing. It's enough to make him say it out loud like a spent wish. 'Just like the good old days.'

THE GOOD OLD DAYS. Not so very old for Mick. Not so very long ago. On stage in America, David crawling between his kneecaps, more voltage than the whole of Las Vegas at his fingertips, bare torso glistening in the spotlight, looking like the dragon-slaying hero of a Wagnerian opera as thousands fainted at his every strum and whammy. Everything a kid from Hull with a headful of Yardbirds could ever dream about. *Good* good old days.

So when did they stop?

In a conversation with Defries in a Japanese hotel room? The stabbing of Trev and Woody's backs? The counting of his 30 pieces of Mainman silver? That last night in Hammersmith, sharing the stage with his hero Jeff Beck when he joined him and David for the encore, all teenage fantasies fulfilled?

When was *The* End?

It goes unnoticed. There's no lingering close-up, no zooming crane shot, no foggy fade to black, no famous last words, no 'Frankly, my dear, I don't give a damn!' Not in real life. The real end always passes without register in mumbles. Missed in the living moment of severance until a time comes – weeks, months, sometimes *years* later – when the sad uncertain mind flicks back its pages to find the missing full stop. And when Mick's time comes, he'll flick back and find it here. The makeshift dressing room of the Marquee's rear studio.

He's not long come off stage, still in his white suit, fingers twiddling a tight roll-up, running his tongue along the paper edge. A few feet away, David, staring in his mirror, wiping the make-up off his cheeks with a cotton pad. This is where it ends. The same place it began.

So fate completes its full circle. From that day in the Marquee to this.

That day. One thousand, three hundred and fifty-five ago. Just over three years and eight months ago. Seventy-one chapters of an odyssey ago.

A Tuesday night in February 1970. There he was in Cambo's Hillman Minx pulling up behind the club in Richmond Mews. Just driven down from Hull where Cambo found him creosoting a rugby pitch then sandblasted his ears telling him about this amazing singer he'd met 'called David Bowie' who needed a guitar player. So Mick agreed to come to London and meet him the night he was headlining the Marquee, the stage where he first clapped eyes on David. The same stage they were on just now, the two of them trying to recreate a spark neither wants to admit has died out.

That night, though, it was only just kindling. There was David, a skinny little thing with curly hair and a 12-string acoustic, and Mick not watching nearly as intently as he was listening. *Songs with melodies that shift chords with confidence,* musical *music with soft edges that could do with some hardening.* And he knew, immediately, he was the one to harden them. First chance he got, a few hours later in Haddon Hall, where for the first time David heard him play. *All instinct, wits and harmonies. Listening for the spaces David doesn't know are there, hoisting silvery light from out of their silent depths.* One thousand, three hundred and fifty-five days ago.

And now look at David. Still a skinny little thing but with spiky hair the colour of a roe deer, fresh from a long day's filming for American television, wiping rouge off his cheekbones.

So much has changed. David. Mick. The world. Partly because they helped change it. In songs, in sound, in fellating guitar strings and an arm around a shoulder on primetime BBC One. God, theirs were the blinding-brightest of good old days. Till they ran out.

The tragedy isn't that David and Mick no longer *want* each other. It's that, for different reasons, they both believe they no longer *need* each other. But that's rock'n'roll. One day it'll save your life, the next it'll break your heart. Like that song Mick's just recorded at the Château in France for his solo album, one of the few good ones on it, and one of the few David spared the charity to help him with. A cover of a modern Italian ballad, the original translating as 'I Would . . . I Wouldn't . . . But If You Want To', until David gave it a new English lyric.

'Music Is Lethal'.

Ain't that the truth. Because here's two more of its casualties. Look at them. Under the roof of the Marquee, back where it began on that first night when David had just come off stage and Cambo tried to introduce him to Mick. But David hardly spoke. Neither did Mick. And a thousand-odd days later here's David sitting at his mirror, and there's Mick standing by the door. Once more, with nothing to say to each other.

Until David stops wiping his face and looks past his reflection. And they suddenly both catch each other's gaze in the glass.

David, a grunt. Mick, a nod.

Then their eyes separate.

David resumes wiping his face. Mick turns and walks. And walks and walks and keeps on walking. Walking with his back to David Bowie. Away from the full stop he never even saw.

EIGHTEEN

STONY GREY NOVEMBER. Grey as the plinth beneath the new statue of Winston in Parliament Square. A fat man hunched in a thick military coat resting on a walking stick, his eyes squinting towards the river, his brow furrowed in what can only be disgust. Even his thick bronze skull can smell it. The putrid stink of rotting glam.

'*That's right! That's right! That's right! That's right!*'

The sound of maggots writhing in Marylebone. In the vocal booth of Audio International Studios, a man named Les who looks like he spins Waltzers for a living but is actually a singer from a band named Mud does the devilish bidding of his songwriting producers. It's the Faustian price his group must pay for selling their souls to Nicky Chinn and Mike Chapman, just as The Sweet and Suzi Quatro did before them, exchanging seven years of Ford Transit toil and Blue Boar breakfasts for silver discs and *Top of the Pops*. It's already got them in the Top 5 with 'Dyna-Mite', which sounds like it could have been written by skipping a needle over the last Sweet single, and very possibly was. Today's tune is called 'Tiger Feet' and it's as scarily contagious as the Black Death. 'It's entertainment, not education,' says Les. So do its 'ChinniChap' writing team, all too aware their critics think most of their songs are garbage. 'But what the hell *is* garbage?' asks Chapman. 'If the kids are buying it, then it's not garbage, is it? I'll tell you what is garbage, and that's a record that never sells. THAT's garbage!'

Everywhere, glam decays in black leather bin liners. See, there's one, stretching over the gaunt body of a 31-year-old impostor born a Bernard, latterly a Shane, but now daring to stand in front of the cameras and degrade himself as 'Alvin Stardust'. *STARDUST!* No, it really isn't enough that glam is dead: now they're shagging the corpse. 'My Coo Ca Choo' commits cold necrophilia to Norman Greenbaum's 'Spirit In The Sky', with the added sacrilege of being made in the same Wimbledon studio where Iggy and the Stooges demoed *Raw Power*. But though he has a passable voice, Alvin doesn't even sing on it. The vocal belongs to its writer and producer, Peter Shelley, who put it out under an alias as the first release on his new Magnet label, not expecting it to be a hit. Or that's his excuse for picking such a moronic pseudonym. But now it's climbing up the chart, Shelley needs a TV puppet. The Shane formerly known as Bernard accepts and thus becomes the bad joke Alvin Stardust incarnate: head-to-toe black leather, matching tight pervy strangler gloves, chunky jewellery, stuck-on sideburns and a costume-party Elvis wig. They say every generation gets the pop stars they deserve: but do the kids of '73 *really* deserve the kind who looks as if he'd ask them to hop in his sidecar for a bag of liquorice as a one-way ticket to their shallow grave?

No wonder Winston grimaces. Never in the field of human music has so much been ruined for so many by so few. And unlike the rest of us, he can never close his eyes or ears to it. Dawn till dusk and all through the night, in rain, fog and thunderstorm, weekdays and weekends, there he stands, gazing across to Big Ben, cursed to spend unblinking eternity watching the giant clock hands twitch the passing of time from which he has no release. Looking out at this land he fought for and won. This, his victory. This, our freedom.

Alvin Fucking Stardust.

The morning dew beads on Winston's bronze eyes like tears. A warm orange sky spreads over the east as the sun rises after 7 a.m. to the clang of men in uniform inspecting manhole covers. In just over four hours' time the Queen and the rest of the royal family will be sat over in the Abbey watching Princess Anne get spliced to a British soldier. And just wouldn't it be the most awful shame if the IRA were to spoil it with another of their bothersome bombs?

While officers keep on poking in hedges and rubbish bins, over in the Palace the anxious bride's immediate thoughts concern only the Englishman coming to fix her hair and the Frenchman to fix her face. Her horsey highness had wanted to use Barbara Daly, last seen backstage at the Marquee powdering the cheeks of David Bowie. But right now she's in Ireland working on the next film by Stanley Kubrick and so, in her place, Anne must bear the lip pencil of a man from a country her great-great-great-great-great-grandfather rode into battle against. No, not, alas, Pierre but one 'Monsieur Olivier'.

As he arranges his brushes *exactement*, carefully separating his stipplers from his blenders, on the other side of Green Park her husband-to-be, Captain Mark Phillips, is still asleep in his suite at the Cavalry Club where last night he, his best man and their haw-hawing chums from the Queen's Dragoon Guards drained some half dozen bottles of the finest champagne. Having woken, washed and dressed in a dark grey pinstripe suit, at 9.30 he clops downstairs to the dining room for his last bachelor's breakfast of coffee, fresh oranges, eggs, bacon, toast and marmalade. One minute to ten, he dabs the corners of his mouth with his napkin, stifles a satisfied belch, and off he trots, secure in the knowledge that in less than two hours he'll be £35,000 richer for having slipped a ring on the finger of a woman who earns fifteen times his army officer's salary.

At seven minutes past, as the Captain and his best man depart the club in an Austin Princess through trafficless streets emptied and cordoned for their exclusive passage, the crowds are already packing tight down The Mall and around the Abbey in Parliament Square. Woollen-coated crowds. Thirsty crowds. Hungry crowds. Thousands up before dawn, buttering bread, slicing tinned ham, boiled eggs, corned beef and cheese, cutting sandwiches in quarters, wrapping in foil or placing in metal tins with pork pies, fruit cake and half-eaten packets of digestive biscuits, filling thermos flasks with sugary tea and milky coffee to sustain them through hour after hour of standing, shivering and strenuous flag-waving. All this only for every crumb, every drop, every scrape of Stork SB to be confiscated by order of Scotland Yard. No bags, no tins, no vacuum flasks. Nothing that might suddenly blow up within a square mile of the

Princess's glass carriage. Not even a bag of crisps. And so they stand and they shiver and they strenuously flag-wave with rumbling stomachs, dry throats and light heads, Winston with his back to them listening to their wan emaciated cheers as Big Ben bongs for elevenses.

An hour later, after all the shitting horses and shiny carriages, after all the fanfares and the hymns, after the babbling dean and the burbling archbishop, after Captain Phillips in full military dress and sword plights Anne his troth, after Anne in her silk wedding dress with pearl-trimmed trumpet sleeves gives him her troth, after everyone is satisfied that all troths are where they should be till death do they part, the dismal dutiful public who haven't yet passed out with malnutrition are still just about upright to weakly flap their Union Jacks as the happy couple trundle past Winston on their way back to the Palace. There they'll dine on a lobster and egg mayonnaise starter mixed with ketchup and sherry, followed by partridge on a bed of lardons, peas and new potatoes, topped off with a cooling peppermint slice of Bombe Glacé Royale. And as the blessed blue bloods savour every mouthful, the starving commoners whose taxes paid for it all stagger off homeward to Spam and tinned fruit cocktail, to the solace of *Dad's Army* and *The World at War*, to penny-pinching lives consumed by fears of the soaring cost of bread and petrol, to tabloid tales of imminent doom about a crashing economy, looming power cuts and the return of the ration coupon. And while Her Majesty's merry subjects lie worrying in the dead of night about how they'll stretch out another week's housekeeping, in a seventeenth-century mansion in Richmond Park two partridge-breathed aristocrats will be consummating their troths. And not that they'll care, though they might think it fitting, when dawn comes around the number 1 record will be 'I Love You Love Me Love' by Gary Glitter. And not that they'll see it, because by then they'll be on a private honeymoon flight to Barbados, but Gary will be singing it on that night's *Top of the Pops* on the very same show Alvin Stardust makes his debut. And as the nation watches Alvin squirming and sneering for his Coo Ca Choo, Winston will still be staring out over Parliament Square, leaning on his stick, wondering how things could possibly be any worse had the bloody Germans won.

★

HOLLYWOOD SEX SCENE. No need for graphic details, but let's just say it's hotter than all hell in these sheets. The kind of sex that acts as an industrial stress test for every spring in the mattress. You think that's great sex Julie Christie and Donald Sutherland are having in *Don't Look Now*? Well, honey, that may be the biggest film pulling in the raincoats in Leicester Square this month, but you stick this pair of rutting goats on screen and the British Board of Film Censorship will have to invent a whole new certificate. Christ! Just the *sound* of it! The banging and slapping and panting and puffing. If these two mated any harder, they'd smash through each other's pelvises and run bucking and thrusting in opposite directions until they air-fucked smack into the hotel walls. They might still yet. Here comes the climax now, shaking the room like the San Andreas Fault. Feel those vibrations! When these two are finally done, someone better check the letters of the Hollywood sign haven't toppled all the way down Mount Lee.

Three! *Ugh!*

Two! *Ah!*

One! *Yes Yes Yes!*

Exploding like a couple of Nagasakis. *AIIIIYEEEEEE!*

And then satisfaction like a bodily supernova, pure and bright and warm and radiating, burning from the inside out, shining from her eyes, her mouth, her finger tips, like she's a blazing beautiful new star freshly superfucked into existence by no less a cosmic power than God himself.

God catches his spent breath and crashes his sweaty head onto the pillow. The body beside him is trembling. God turns to look at her. She looks at him, smiling. No, laughing. A wild ecstatic out-of-body laugh like nothing she's laughed before, like she can't even breathe, but she can't stop herself. Until, at last, she manages to speak.

'OH,' laughs Angie, 'MY FUCKING *GOD!*'

Her fucking god. Only a few hours ago he was waiting for her backstage the moment the cameras stopped prerecording at NBC's Burbank studios where Angie, the anthropologist Ashley Montagu, comedian Joan Rivers and TV host Dinah Shore were the guests on today's *The Tonight Show Starring Johnny Carson*. She'd wanted Johnny to announce her as 'Jipp Jones' but had to settle for being Mrs Bowie, famous rock wife, there to promote David's edition of *The Midnight Special*, which is being broadcast directly after it on the same channel. Angie had been booked to talk about it on his behalf, warned that if she made a bad impression, then she risked losing at least 30 per cent of David's potential audience who might switch over in disgust to a bedroom farce with Doris Day or the late-night horror *Son of Frankenstein*. This was only after she turned up for rehearsal in a scanty satin top with two pink clamshells covering her tits which they made her remove. For the final taping she changed into a lavender chiffon dress worn by her mother. The dress currently lying somewhere on her bedroom floor where it was strewn in an unzipping frenzy just before her scorchingly handsome fucking god made her cum like . . .

'WONDER WOMAN!'

Her other reason for being here in Hollywood. 'Jipp Jones' is doing a screen test for the lead in a new ABC TV pilot of *Wonder Woman*, based on the famous DC superhero. Angie's so enthusiastic she's come prepared to wow the producers with special glamour portraits of herself in a homemade Wonder Woman costume complete with tiara, black wig, starry hot pants and lasso. Which, as it turns out, is a complete waste of time, cotton and camera film.

The script reads more like a cheap James Bond-style spy thriller. The main character of Diana Prince is no superpowered Amazonian daughter of Zeus but an undercover secret agent working as a secretary who sometimes slips into a fancy tracksuit to fight bad guys with a bit of kung fu. There's no gold-and-ruby tiara, no Lasso of Truth and, for Angie, no loss when she doesn't get the part. In the end they give it to an established TV actress, Cathy Lee Crosby, who is everything the pilot demands. No wonder, just woman.

Still, at least it got Angie to Hollywood and into bed with her fucking god. Smouldering beside her now, hot as a newly crashed meteor, his dark hair sweeping back from his clammy forehead, tumbling down to his skinny bony shoulders and softly heaving chest. With that face of his, a face like the sound of a thick leather belt being whipped out of tight trouser loops and dropped to the floor with a buckly clank. A scream-if-you-wanna-go-faster face hewn from nights such as this breaking all speed limits. A face that makes her glad that she's a woman and that she's here, 5,000 miles from . . .

. . . Hell, what time is it anyway? The early hours of Saturday morning in LA? Which means it'll be coming up for lunchtime in London. Ha! *London.* She can picture it in her mind's eye. David, round about now waking up in their bed in Oakley Street. Or someone else's? Wonder with whom? Amanda? Ava? Laurita? Marianne? *Lulu?* Ah, *who* cares! He might as well fuck the damned lot of them, all at once. Because the stakes of this whole open marriage fandango have suddenly been upped. A *lot* higher.

Oh, baby! Just *wait* till David finds out. And wait till she tells her friend Pierre!

'Your *favoreet* male face! Oui, Pierre! Je suis fucking Mickey Finn!'

'*NOT THE ORGASM DEATH.*' David hurriedly turns the pages of the black jacketed paperback, eyes scanning each line with machine-like speed, repeatedly sniffing like he's trying to snort the text up into his brain as fast as he possibly can. It's a speedy, snorty sort of book from a pile given to him a few days ago by a writer from the London office of *Rolling Stone* magazine. The others are speedy and snorty too, but then most books by William Burroughs are, especially this one, *Nova Express,* part of his experimental 'cut-up trilogy' aimed at making every sentence as comprehensively nonsensical as possible. It's the only one David's managed to flick through so far, which wouldn't be a problem if it weren't for the fact that any minute now his doorbell is going to ring and standing on the doorstep will be William Burroughs. Here on the understanding he'll be invited in for a riveting conversation with David Bowie, the great English pop star, about, among other things, just how much he loves the work of the great American beat writer William Burroughs.

The doorbell rings.

Standing on the doorstep is William Burroughs.

He's a thin, ageing man in a chequered suit, dark tie and black fedora, with the drinker's face of an Irish bookmaker not unknown to some of the boys on the Meat Rack down the Dilly. In practice, it's more a prescription opiate face fond of vodka and Coke and the occasional puff on a cigarette dipped in tincture of cannabis. Beside him is the same *Rolling Stone* writer who set this rendezvous up, a tall American named

Craig with a bubble of curly hair, a black jacket, white jumper, dark trousers and scuffed white loafers. Behind them, a black cab chugs away after its short journey from William's flat in Duke Street, St James's, just round the corner from Tramp, where he never sets foot, and Fortnum & Mason, where he buys his coffee and salted crackers.

Only a few months shy of 60, William's knowledge of David is only marginally better than David's of William. He's only heard two of his songs, 'Five Years' and 'Starman', though thanks to Craig he has read the lyric sheets of his last few albums, and what he read he liked enough to agree to meet David for the sake of sharing what dialogue emerges with the readers of *Rolling Stone*.

The door opens with a waft of warm spice and the vision of a striking Asian girl with a lemon-yellow Sassoon crop. Daniella welcomes them inside, leading up the stairs to the living room. A few minutes pass before David, having speedily snorted as much *Nova Express* as he can, joins them: his clothes loose and casual; his grin taut and nervous. Craig formally introduces them. William, his face every bit as unreadable as his books, nods and sits down as the smell that greeted them suddenly intensifies with the arrival of salvers of steaming Jamaican red snapper, rice, avocados stuffed with prawns and the first of several bottles of Beaujolais.

'Help yourself,' says David, lighting a Marlboro. William digs inside his jacket pocket, pulls out a Senior Service and does the same. David pours the wine and pinches a prawn. William doesn't touch a morsel. Craig's tape recorder spins. On the far wall, like the naughty kids at the back of school assembly, a mute audience of Jimmy Deans.

'I'm an awful liar,' says David.

'I am too,' says William in a deep Midwest drawl like a starting chainsaw.

'I don't exactly lie,' corrects David. 'I change my mind all the time.'

William nods and makes a sage comment about Hitler. 'He never changed his mind.'

The framed Jimmy Deans quietly snigger.

David coughs, sniffs, puffs and decides he'll risk bringing up *Nova Express*. 'It really reminded me of *Ziggy Stardust*,' he lies, desperately hoping William doesn't ask him about anything that happens beyond page 50.

'Hmm,' hmms William, who luckily doesn't.

'I'm going to be putting it into a theatrical performance,' David continues. 'There's 40 scenes in it . . .' *Sniff.* '. . . and it would be nice if the characters and the actors learned the scenes and we all shuffled them around in a hat the afternoon of the performance . . .' *Sniff.* '. . . and just performed it as the scenes come out. I got this all from you, Bill . . .'

'Hmm,' hmms William, absorbing the sudden familiarity of Bill.

'. . . so it would change every night.'

'Hmm. That's a very good idea. Visual cut-up in a different sequence.'

'Cut-ups, yes . . .' *Sniff.* '. . . I'd like to use them more.'

'Hmm. So could you explain this Ziggy Stardust image of yours? From what I can see it has to do with the world being on the eve of destruction within five years.'

David's brain clenches tight like a fist. Explain Ziggy Stardust? He's been trying to do that for the last two years. It was simple, once. Just a make-believe rock star. That's all. Just a costume to wear on stage and the right songs to make it dance. But then everyone got the costume and the songs mixed up: David dressed as Ziggy and sang 'Starman'; Starman became Ziggy; Ziggy became an alien. Two plus two equals five. Only now that Ziggy's as good as 'dead' the arithmetic no longer matters. So David can sit here adding and subtracting any old wacky bollocks. Which with everything that's just zoomed up his sinuses, *Nova Express* included, comes easy as turning on a tap.

'Yes, it's five years to the end of the earth,' begins David. 'The kids have given up on rock'n'roll . . .' *Sniff.* '. . . because there's no longer any electricity.'

Ziggy, he explains, is an ex-rock star who predicts the coming of an amazing spaceman who will save earth, only the 'Starman' he's talking about isn't a he but a they.

'Black hole jumpers . . .' *Sniff.* '. . . called the Infinites.'

Who by pure cosmic chance land in New York's Greenwich Village.

'One looks like Brando . . .' *Sniff.* '. . . and one is called Queenie the Infinite Fox.'

Having predicted their arrival, Ziggy is revered as a messiah-like prophet with a huge following of disciples.

'But when the Infinites arrive . . .' *Sniff.* '. . . they take bits of Ziggy to make themselves real . . .' *Sniff.* '. . . because in their original state they're antimatter . . .' *Sniff.* '. . . and can't exist in our world.'

'Hmm,' hmms William, now genuinely intrigued.

'So they tear Ziggy to pieces . . .' *Sniff.* '. . . and he dies, to make themselves visible . . .' *Sniff.* '. . . it's a science-fiction fantasy of today and that's what literally blew my head off when I read *Nova Express* . . .' *Sniff.* '. . . which was written in 1961!'

'Hmm.'

'Maybe we are the Rodgers and Hammerstein of the Seventies, Bill.'

'Hmmmyyyes,' hmms William positively. 'I can believe that. The parallels are definitely there. Hmm. It sounds good.'

Craig's recorder suddenly clicks to a stop. The conversation pauses while he fiddles turning his tape over.

William leans forward over the avocados.

'You know,' he says, eyeballing David with a grandfatherly smile, 'the best way to take cocaine is to make sure you've clipped all your nose hairs first.'

THEY'RE TOO BUSY thinking about the needle to lock the cubicle door and too busy tapping veins to notice they're being watched. By the time they do, they're too high to care. The teenage schoolboy staring at them isn't alarmed, just fascinated. He's never seen anyone mainline heroin before and the last place he expected to is the gents toilet in Biba. A stunned blink commits the scene to memory like a long exposure before he leaves them to it. The next time he sees Johnny Thunders and Jerry Nolan is later that evening in the Rainbow Room.

Up on the stage.

One year after they first came here as five and went home as four, the New York Dolls are back. Now five again with a new junkie drummer and a debut album to 'redeem the social outcasts of Britain'. So far it's got them on the cover of *Melody Maker* with Thunders in a swastika armband, a four-page advert in *Gay News* and mailbags dripping with bile after daring to alleviate the tedium of another Tuesday night's *Old Grey Whistle Test* with the juiciest pouting since Marilyn Monroe blew 'boop-boop-de-boop'. To their few fans and many foes, the Dolls defy description. 'We've been called glitter kids, street punks, a fag band,' lists singer David Johansen. 'But I never wore glitter in my life. I mean it probably gives you cancer, y'know.'

It's also got them the honour of being the first band to play Biba's Rainbow Room, the first to shoot up in its toilets and the first to be arrested by store security for trying to switch price tags on a woman's fake leopard-trim coat. They play two nights here with an injured bass player still recovering from a jealous chick's botched attempt to chop his hand off in his sleep. The first show they demand 40 bottles of champagne for their dressing room. Add two parts heroin and they play like it was 80.

'We just bash it out however it comes,' brags Johansen. 'The kids don't have to think about us. They can just dance.'

But there's not a lot of dancing in Biba, nor a lot of bodies, just a couple of hundred on both nights despite the inclusion of a free meal in the £2.50 ticket. Last year, the Dolls made the mistake of coming over before anyone was ready. This year, they're a good six or seven months too late. Somewhere between, the battle for the soul of glam, which they might have won for its original cause to strangle rock machismo with a feather boa, has been lost. The gloating victors are Mud and Alvin and Gary and Suzi and every other suffocating carpetbagger tramping over its grave on the path to *Crackerjack*. It'd be nice to believe there's a parallel universe where the Dolls' album knocks *Sing It Again Rod* off number 1, Pan's People are dancing to 'Personality Crisis' and *Jackie* are vox popping schoolgirls what they'd make Johnny Thunders for his tea. 'Bangers and smack!' But England 1973 isn't it. Two days after their second Biba gig, Pan's People are dancing to David Essex, *Jackie* are vox popping schoolgirls how they would spend £100 – 'Plastic surgery: I hate my nose!' – and the number 1 album for the fifth week running is *Pin Ups* by their famous pal who lives a five-minute limo away but still never came to see them.

Maybe over in that parallel universe the Dolls are already on their way to a block-solid sell-out week at Wembley, with David Bowie as their opening support act. Yeah. That'd be sweet.

Because in this one they never stand together on a British stage again.

NINETEEN

THE EYES OF JIMMY DEAN SEE IT ALL. The screwing, the snorting, the whole sleazy circus. The furtive looks, the lapping tongues, the writhing bodies, the bobbing heads, the pumping buttocks, the slapping thighs, the sheepish excuse-mes up the stairs, the ins and outs, the ups and downs, the white vials and tiny spoons, the hashish eyes and the mandie smiles, every intimacy and every exhibition. From David's wall, Jimmy sees it all.

Like he's watching a film about a famous rock'n'roll star hiding from the world in his psychedelic West London pad. A strange film, full of sex and drugs and cameos from Mick Jagger. A film Jimmy doesn't know the name of but David does, because it's the one he saw over two years ago on a Leicester Square cinema screen, only now it's happening in his sitting room. Now it's his reality.

David is living *Performance*.

He's even got the same pug-faced gangsters in his house. Johnny Bindon, a genuine villain who did two years for aggravated assault before he wound up playing one of Harry Flowers' mob, 'Moody'. He still spends most of his time bit-part acting to thuggish type between ducking and diving around the King's Road, beating the shit out of blokes with his frighteningly quick fists and boggling birds with his freakishly large penis. David doesn't remember personally inviting the man everyone calls

'Biffo' over the threshold of Oakley Street, but here he is in his sofa pit, joint in his swollen-side-of-beef hand, a dildo strapped to his concrete forehead, laughing his 'laugh or I'll snap yer spine in 'alf' bullyboy laugh with Angie and Dana and whoever else happens to be sliding around the silver cushions. One day maybe William Burroughs. One day Amanda. One day Marianne. One day Mick and Bianca. But every day Jimmy watching him with those eyes. Those cruel vain empty eyes. It's why David put him on his wall in the first place. 'It is the very emptiness of James Dean that makes him so appealing,' he says. 'Try and find a personality in *that*.' Then gently erodes his own with another stiff sniff of mental quicklime.

Sometimes Jimmy can't see at all for his eyes trembling with the G-force from the stereo speakers, the whole room a juddering blur of funky Jamaica during hours when David can't play the seismic skank of Toots and the Maytals loud enough for his whizzing head's liking. *'I'm gonna sit right down,'* swears Toots, but Jimmy's only gravitational concern is the rattling picture hook in the wall behind him.

When the music finally stops, the TV usually switches on. Jimmy's eyes now blinded by lockstepping swastikas, David transfixed by what he thinks looks exactly like a rock star greeting his adoring fans. After picking up a state-of-the-art video recorder in Japan he's able to tape Leni Riefenstahl's *Triumph of the Will* off BBC Two for keeps. Three nights later, the same buttons click when the Beeb shows *Barbarella*. And if the TV goes off and once more becomes the dulled mirror of Orwell's telescreen following David's every move as intently as Jimmy's eyes, he might turn his film projector on. He's been collecting prints of old movies, even *Rebel Without a Cause*, and Jimmy has to hang there admiring David admiring Jimmy's lack of personality as he leaps from a car before it falls off a cliff. And if it's not cars tumbling into the sea, it's skeletons. The sword-swiping dead of a teenage favourite, *Jason and the Argonauts*. Often just him, and Jimmy, curtains drawn, reels whirring, his nasal cavity crackling like indoor fireworks, slumped there transfixed by harpies, hydras and ancient Greek heroes.

Just like Howard Hughes. Still lying naked on his paper towels on the ninth floor of the Inn on the Park as his own projector spins.

Two men, not two miles apart, with their drugs and their flickering fantasies. Alone in their outer spaces.

JIMMY DEAN, JIMMY DEAN. Everywhere, Jimmy Dean. In David Bowie's sitting room. On Iggy's belt buckle. In a Top 10 record by David Essex. On the backdrop behind Paul Nicholas and Elaine Paige, the new Danny and Sandy in *Grease* in Covent Garden, and on its poster outside. In the photo racks of Malcolm McLaren's rock'n'roll Mecca on the King's Road. On the front cover of the *NME* with the headline 'THIS MAN STARTED IT ALL'.

And scowling from another picture frame on the wall of a newly refurbished first-floor office opposite Milbanke Travel on New Bond Street. The exact same black-and-white image on the stage of *Grease*: Jimmy looking down into the lens in a chunky rollneck jumper, chin cocked to one side, bags under black eyes challenging the universe to try to make his sulky chops crack a smile. The photo was taken 19 years ago when Dean was 23. He'd be dead at 24, just as he wished. 'Live fast, die young and leave a good-looking corpse.' Only Jimmy's corpse didn't look so hot: his bloody torso crushed behind his Porsche's steering wheel in a head-on collision which broke his neck on the last day of September 1955. It was Marc Bolan's eighth birthday.

And 18 years later, here he is hanging in his new office.

The eyes of Jimmy Dean see it all, but there's not nearly so much to see in Mayfair as in Chelsea. Just a bright room with large roller-blinded windows, a telephone, a rotary fan, a large fibreglass rocking horse, a rattan chair, walls full of silver and gold discs, a promotional cardboard cut-out for the new T. Rex *Great Hits* album that isn't selling and his own reflection in the far full-length wall mirror. And, when business demands, his deathday birthday boy, leaning back against woven wicker in a black suit, a pink shirt, an itchy nose and a glass of vodka, staring straight back at Jimmy.

Marc says he put him there so he can look up and remind himself 'what not to be'. If he means a fucked-up narcissist, he's failing.

You can see it in Marc's eyes. They're not pretty anymore. They're dark, heavy, bad man's eyes, all the darker and heavier now that he's chopped his hair short, leaving his bloating face nowhere to hide. It's as if the picture of Jimmy is his portrait of Dorian Gray in reverse, infecting Marc with its toxic emptiness – if it weren't for the fact the distorting sins are entirely Marc's own.

'*It's not been Bolan's year, really. We hear that moon and June don't rhyme anymore.*'

The pop gossip columns will twist their knives. But none as hard as Marc twisted his. Wasn't it six months ago he told the press that marriage was the thing that kept him sane?

'I'd have opted out years ago without June,' he'd said, 'there's no doubt about that.'

Yes, he did. And yes, a few weeks later he left her for one of his new 'black chick backing singers from America' named Gloria.

It was June who moved out of their £80-a-week secure apartment near Marble Arch. She left him the furniture and the fridge but not his vegetarian diet. Now Gloria's moved in, Marc's got his nutrition down to the four essentials. Roast chicken, vodka, champagne, cocaine.

To his imminent divorce papers from June he can add those of Tony Visconti. A long handwritten letter telling Marc in the plainest terms possible he's a monstrous arsehole Tony can no longer bring himself to work with. Marc can't care enough to reply. He's just been finishing the new T. Rex album without Tony, and now that he's gone, it sounds exactly how Marc wants it to sound. Like roast chicken, vodka, champagne and cocaine, some higher in the mix than others. Besides, the three T. Rex singles of '73 have been like a bad hand at darts, each hitting lower than the last. If he won't blame himself, he can always blame Tony. He's definitely not going to blame his fans.

'The kids know where I'm at,' sniffs Marc. 'They don't feel rejected. They associate with me much more than they will with David Bowie or anyone like that because they've put themselves apart.'

Not like Marc. OK, so he *still* hasn't played a single gig in Britain all year, but at least he's now a poster inside special boxes of Shredded Wheat. And he's still on the cover of *Mirabelle*, looking swollen, doped and demonic, his pinkie wiggling tacky jewellery from H. Samuel that isn't even his in a competition to 'WIN MARC'S DIAMOND RING!' No, you wouldn't see the aloof likes of David Bowie doing that. That's why Marc's still who he says he is. 'A street punk.' That's why he's got Jimmy on his wall, to remind him what not to be. A dead teen idol in a crumpled car.

'When the almighty hand hits you, he wants you and he takes you,' he says aloud to Jimmy. 'I don't care – it's pre-ordained.' *Sniff.* 'My body isn't important.' *Sniff.* 'My spirit is fine, that's what matters.' *Sniff.* 'I've gotten to like him, this silly little street punk Marc Bolan.' *Sniff.* 'A lot I don't like about him.' *Sniff.* 'A lot I hate.' *Sniff.* 'But I know my own shortcomings.'

And if that won't make Jimmy laugh, nothing will.

It's in short supply this Christmas. Laughter, that is. Below them, the street is crammed with nervous shoppers buying as much as they can in the tense hope they'll make it home to peel the sprouts without running into any car bombs. The odds are even: just the 61 people injured in blasts so far this week. The IRA have even started planting bombs in West End cinemas. Possibly why sales of alcohol have now risen by 40 per cent. Given the choice, people have decided they'd much sooner die of Cossack vodka consumption.

Marc's cocktail cabinet is living proof. He'll be staying at home this Christmas, with no plans other than to maybe pop into the Odeon round the corner from his flat where they're playing that new Sinbad film with special effects by Ray Harryhausen, the same guy who did *Jason and the Argonauts*. Griffins, centaurs and hot Arabian chicks in skimpy bikinis. He'll dig that.

Then it's off to the Bahamas with Gloria for New Year. It's going to be a better one, 1974. He can feel it in his nostrils. Next year he's going to get back on the road, back to the kids, back on top, where he belongs. *Yeah! The world's number 1 street punk!*

Marc chucks the last of his vodka down his neck. He strolls sniffing towards the door with a pat to the rocking horse, sending it gently swaying, not bothering to glance goodbye at the picture on his wall.

He doesn't need to. Jimmy has already seen too much.

SO HERE IT IS. The end of 1973. Only a few hours to go before it's put out of its misery. And didn't December save the worst till last? An oil blockade in the Middle East causing a knock-on national catastrophe. Stresses on coal production and another miners' dispute. Pan Am flights grounded because they've run out of fuel. Panic buying at the pumps and hiking petrol costs. Voltage shortages at power stations, blackouts and power cuts. The lights on the Christmas tree in Trafalgar Square switched on for one night, then switched off for ten days. The government's festive gift of the three-day-week with fears as many as five million will soon be drawing dole. A post office embargo on parcels delivered to London and a British Rail ban on the transport of perishable goods including Christmas turkeys. The rail unions on a go-slow and no trains on Sundays. Record companies in crisis because vinyl and cardboard supplies have dwindled. No *NME* on the newsstands because of a printers' strike. All TV channels forced to shut down at half ten every night. Over £800 million lost on the Stock Exchange. A £270 million trade gap. Steel output slashed. The biggest drop in living standards in 20 years. Record inflation. The *Mirror* asking 'IS <u>EVERYBODY</u> GOING MAD?' *The Sun* screaming 'YOU'VE NEVER HAD IT SO BAD'. The *Mail* glumly understating '*the start of 1974 is going to be disagreeable*'. Just like Slade have been warning us all month.

'*It's only just beguuu-uuu-uuun!*'

Hark the herald angels weep. In ballads of dead film stars, love lying bleeding and Emerald Cities turned to dust – the number 1 album this Christmas, *Goodbye Yellow Brick Road*. Elton is the ghost of sadness present whatever record speed you choose. The killer blow in this week's Top 20 singles isn't one of his, but it's still his doing. A French ballad, sung by his Yorkshire-born friend, released on his label and with his production. 'Amoureuse' is for the grown-ups sitting alone after the Slade kids have all gone to bed, wallowing in Beefeater gin and an unhappiness so profound it's like '*the rainfall of another planet*'. When life on Earth is empty cupboards, candles and the queue outside the Labour Exchange, who this New Year doesn't feel like Kiki Dee?

Howard Hughes, maybe. Now feeling the sunshine of another continent. Or would be if he wasn't still imprisoned behind closed curtains in a new hotel suite in the Bahamas. After one year in the Inn on the Park, he upped and left last week in a DC-9, taking his staff, his syringes and his film projector with him.

Leaving behind a London reeling in its own 24-frame-a-second madness. The sex of *Hot and Blue*, the violence of *Magnum Force*, and horror after unbearable horror. At the closest cinema to Buckingham Palace, the Metropole in Victoria Street, a new double bill pairs two films nobody should ever be allowed to watch back to back if they're not already certified insane: *The Wicker Man* and *Don't Look Now*. Pagan sacrifice versus psycho dwarves. In a contest for the grimmest ending in the history of folding seats, this is a one-all draw.

At present, they're only halfway through. The onscreen sun is setting as the first matinee audience wince to the death screams of Sergeant Howie, some in the tragic misunderstanding the film coming up straight after it can't possibly be any bleaker. Happy New Year.

Outside the cinema, 1973's last hours of daylight cling to a clear day with a sting of frost. In cars and cafés the radios play 'Merry Xmas Everybody' like the final Hokey Cokey before the boot comes stamping on the human face, forever. Perhaps as soon as the stroke of midnight.

Right now, only the stroke of mid-afternoon. In Beckenham, a bored record department sales assistant plays with her sticker gun. In Ruislip, a girl called Brenda and her mate, Carol, are listening to *Pin Ups* as they paint their nails with the 'Poppy Ice' and 'Crimson Sorbet' they gave each other for Christmas. In Kilburn, the jars are draining in Biddy Mulligan's like the bells have already rung. In Biba, the Rainbow Room ceiling glows pastel pink above the scrape of spoon through ginger syllabub. In the depths of the Thames, sewage swims with the last rotting specks of Paul Raven's coffin.

And in a private upstairs dining room off The Strand, all eyes are on David. He has been ceremonially summoned to the regal lattice-windowed splendour of Rules restaurant before an invited audience of journalists and staff from Mainman and RCA, here to commemorate the end of his year as Britain's most successful albums artist. Sat like a Bond villain at the head of a long table, he wears a single hoop earring and the new suit Freddie made him for Christmas: its bolero cut inspired by the ones worn by Carmen, the jacket embroidered on the back with a character from a book David's been reading about the outlawed Russian underground press of 'Political Progressive Pornography' – an image of a semi-naked Amazonian superheroine drawn as a cross between '*mongoloid features and Brigitte Bardot*'.

She's called 'Octobriana', a name he now wants Amanda to adopt instead of 'Dooshenka' when he launches her pop career. David mentions her briefly in passing today between forkfuls of broccoli and the odd itchy sniff as he lists his forthcoming plans for 1974. He's also been producing an album for Ava and the Astronettes, donating some new tracks of his own, padding the rest with covers of the Beach Boys and Bruce Springsteen. And, still very much top of his agenda, his *1984* and *Ziggy* musicals. 'Both finished,' he says, 'it's just a matter of deciding how to do them.'

The big moment of presentation arrives. Cameras flash as David is handed a special frame of six discs marking his six albums still in the chart at the same time: *Space Oddity*, *The Man Who Sold The World*, *Hunky Dory*, *Ziggy Stardust*, *Aladdin Sane* and *Pin Ups*. Ready to mount on his living-room wall beside Jimmy Dean, should he choose. Which he won't.

He holds it, grinning, gums twitching, bared teeth clenched.

He says, 'I don't know what to say.'

In the frame, six other David Bowies blink back at him. Neither do they.

He says, 'I feel like a rock'n'roll star.'

In his pocket, as evidence, the small silvery spoon that last brushed his septum an hour ago.

Then he laughs and says, 'At least it keeps the kids on the streets.' And the whole table smiles back at him.

Half a mile away, they still are. Kids on the streets as the sun sets over the Dilly. Every day a little older, every day that much less innocent, every day that slimmer the chance of buying it back.

Nothing has changed in the lives hung up to dry on the Meat Rack. Only the cost of their pills, the faces of their 'steamers' and the advertising hoardings around the Circus. Like that new long and thin one over there on the sharp corner of Haymarket and Coventry Street. A line drawing of a man in a cobweb leotard with two dummy hands over his breast, and a caption in thick, fat, mostly lower-case lettering.

it looks like
Christmas
love on ya!
Bowie

And doesn't it just look like Christmas in the eyes of this old steamer creeping up the Tube steps, sizing tonight's choices up and down, wondering which to offer a hot meal, a warm bed and his damp fiver. Some, the coldest, the hungriest, the bronchial, trying hard to catch his nod. But others too detached in their amphetamine daze, already lost in the outer spaces. Just leaning there, staring up at David blocking out the stars, drowning in the rainfall of another planet.

BOWIE**DISCOGRAPHY**73

April   **'Drive-In Saturday'**
b/w 'Round And Round'
RCA Victor 2352. Reached number 3 in the first week of May.

Aladdin Sane
'Watch That Man', 'Aladdin Sane (1913–1938–197?)',
'Drive-In Saturday', 'Panic In Detroit', 'Cracked Actor' / 'Time',
'The Prettiest Star', 'Let's Spend The Night Together',
'The Jean Genie', 'Lady Grinning Soul'
*RCA Victor LSP 4852. David's first number 1 album, entering at
the top in the first week of May and staying there for five weeks. Later
certified as the UK's best-selling album of 1973.*

May   **IGGY AND THE STOOGES**
Raw Power
'Search And Destroy', 'Gimme Danger', 'Your Pretty Face Is
Going To Hell', 'Penetration' / 'Raw Power', 'I Need Somebody',
'Shake Appeal', 'Death Trip'
CBS S65586. Produced by Iggy but 'mixed by' David and Iggy.

June   **'Life On Mars?'**
b/w 'The Man Who Sold The World'
RCA Victor 2316. Reached number 3 in early July.

September **'The Laughing Gnome'**
b/w 'The Gospel According To Tony Day'
Deram DM123. Repressing of single first released in April 1967 (and never deleted), peaking at number 6 in early October.

'Sorrow'
b/w 'Amsterdam'
RCA Victor 2424. Reached number 3 in late October.

October **Pin Ups**
'Rosalyn', 'Here Comes The Night', 'I Wish You Would', 'See Emily Play', 'Everything's Alright', 'I Can't Explain' / 'Friday On My Mind', 'Sorrow', 'Don't Bring Me Down', 'Shapes Of Things', 'Anyway, Anyhow, Anywhere', 'Where Have All The Good Times Gone'
RCA Victor RS1003. Entered at number 1 in the last week of October, staying there for five weeks. While it safely beat its rival album released the same day, Bryan Ferry's These Foolish Things *(entering at its peak of number 5), ironically* Pin Ups *was eventually knocked off number 1 in early December by* Stranded *– Bryan's third album with Roxy Music.*

BOWIESOURCES73

VARIOUS AUTHOR INTERVIEWS conducted for the *Bowie Odyssey* series; for this book particular thanks to the contributions of the late John 'Hutch' Hutchinson (interviewed in 2019) and Mark Pritchett. Additional information from this author's past interviews with David Johansen, Arthur Kane and Sylvain Sylvain of the New York Dolls (2004), Iggy Pop (2010) and Noddy Holder (2018).

The memoirs of Angie Bowie, *Free Spirit* (Mushroom Books, 1981) and *Backstage Passes: Life on the Wild Side with David Bowie* (with Patrick Carr, Putnam, 1993); David Bowie's own words as included in Mick Rock's photography collection *Moonage Daydream: The Life and Times of Ziggy Stardust* (Universe, 2005); Amanda Lear, *My Life with Dalí* (Virgin, 1985); Lulu, *I Don't Want to Fight* (Little, Brown, 2002); Geoff MacCormack with foreword by David Bowie, *From Station to Station: Travels with Bowie 1973–1976* (Genesis, 2007); Robin Mayhew, *Ambition* (self-published, 2016); Cherry Vanilla, *Lick Me: How I Became Cherry Vanilla* (Chicago Review Press, 2010); Tony Visconti, *Bowie, Bolan and the Brooklyn Boy* (HarperCollins, 2007); Woody Woodmansey, *Spider from Mars: My Life with Bowie* (Sidgwick & Jackson, 2016); and Tony Zanetta, as detailed in his and Henry Edwards' *Stardust: The David Bowie Story* (McGraw-Hill, 1986). Also, the recollections of Bandō Tamasaburō as published in the February 2017 issue of *Fujingaho* magazine.

The chronology of Bowie historian Kevin Cann's *Any Day Now: David Bowie: The London Years 1947–74* (Adelita, 2010).

Other works: Joe Ambrose, *Gimme Danger: The Story of Iggy Pop* (Omnibus Press, 2004); Donald L. Bartlett and James B. Steele, *Howard Hughes: His Life & Madness* (André Deutsch, 2003); *Berlitz World-Wide Phrase Book* (Berlitz, 1962); William S. Burroughs, *Nova Express* (Jonathan Cape, 1966); Kevin Cann with Chris Duffy, *Duffy Bowie: Five Sessions* (ACC Editions, 2014); Ossie Clark, *The Ossie Clark Diaries* (Bloomsbury, 1998); Neil Cossar, *David Bowie: I Was There* (Red Planet, 2017); Peter & Leni Gillman, *Alias David Bowie* (New English Library, 1987); Gary Glitter (with Lloyd Bradley), *Leader: The Autobiography* (Ebury Press, 1991); Johnny Gold, *Tramp's Gold* (Robson, 2001); Mervyn Harris, *The Dilly Boys: Male Prostitution in Piccadilly* (Croom Helm, 1973); Jerry Hopkins, *Bowie* (Macmillan, 1985); L. Ron Hubbard, *Dianetics: The Original Thesis* (S.P.O., 1970); Barbara Hulanicki, *From A to Biba* (Hutchinson, 1983); Dylan Jones, *David Bowie: A Life* (Preface, 2017); Janie Jones with Carol Clerk, *The Devil and Miss Jones* (Smith Gryphon, 1993); Steve Jones with Ben Thompson, *Lonely Boy: Tales from a Sex Pistol* (William Heinemann, 2016); Nick Kent, *Apathy for the Devil: A 70s Memoir* (Faber, 2010); Alex Kerr, *Lost Japan: Last Glimpse of Beautiful Japan* (Penguin, 2015); Wendy Leigh, *Bowie: The Biography* (Gallery Books, 2014); Norma Levy, *I, Norma Levy* (Blond & Briggs, 1973); Cliff McLenehan, *Marc Bolan: 1947– 1977 A Chronology* (Helter Skelter, 2002); Chris O'Leary, *Rebel Rebel: All the Songs of David Bowie from '64 to '76* (Zero Books, 2015); George Orwell, *Nineteen Eighty-Four* (Secker & Warburg, 1949); Mark Paytress, *Bolan: The Rise and Fall of a 20th Century Superstar* (Omnibus Press, 2006); Nicholas Pegg, *The Complete David Bowie* (expanded and updated edition) (Titan Books, 2016); Mick Rock with foreword by David Bowie, *Glam! An Eyewitness Account* (Omnibus Press, 2005); Peter Sadecky, *Octobriana and the Russian Underground* (Tom Stacey, 1971); Christopher Sandford, *Bowie: Loving the Alien* (Little, Brown, 1996); George Tremlett, *The David Bowie Story* (Futura, 1974); Paul Trynka, *Iggy Pop: Open Up and Bleed* (Sphere, 2007) and *Starman: David Bowie: The Definitive Biography* (Little, Brown, 2011); Alwyn W. Turner, *Biba: The Biba Experience* (ACC Editions, 2004); Judith Watt, *Ossie Clark 1965–74* (V&A Publications, 2003).

Key period broadcasts and theatrical releases referenced: *The Goodies* (BBC, 1973), episode 'Superstar', directed by Jim Franklin, written by Tim Brooke-Taylor, Graeme Garden and Bill Oddie; *Live and Let Die* (Eon Productions, 1973), directed by Guy Hamilton, screenplay by Tom Mankiewicz.

Period newspapers and magazines. National: *Daily Mirror, Daily Express, Daily Mail, Daily Telegraph, Guardian, News of the World, Nova, Observer, Radio Times, The Sun, Sunday Express, Sunday Mirror, Sunday People, Sunday Times* (and *Magazine*), *The Times, TV Times, Vogue.* Regional: *Beckenham Journal, Bridlington Free Press, Birmingham Evening Mail, Courier and Advertiser* (Dundee), *Coventry Evening Telegraph, Croydon Advertiser, Daily Record* (Scotland), *Evening Argus* (Brighton), *Evening Chronicle* (Newcastle), *Evening Echo* (Bournemouth), *Evening Express* (Aberdeen), *Evening News* (Edinburgh), *Evening News* (London), *Evening News* (Worcester), *Evening Post* (Bristol), *Evening Post* (Chatham), *Evening Post* (Leeds), *Evening Sentinel* (Stoke-on-Trent), *Evening Standard* (London), *Evening Telegraph and Post* (Dundee), *Evening Times* (Glasgow), *Hammersmith News and Fulham Post, Hull and Yorkshire Times* (City Edition), *Illustrated London News, The Journal* (Newcastle), *Kensington News and Post, Kilburn Times, Liverpool Echo, Oxford Mail, Press and Journal* (Aberdeen), *Romford and Hornchurch Recorder and Brentwood Review, Salisbury Journal, Shepherd's Bush Gazette and Hammersmith Post, Spalding Guardian, The Star* (Sheffield), *Sunday Mail* (Scotland), *Sunday Post* (Scotland), *Surrey Advertiser* (Guildford).

Pop/rock and teenage: *Disc, Fabulous 208, Honey & Vanity Fair, Jackie, Look-In, Melody Maker, Mirabelle, Music Scene, Music Week, New Musical Express, 19, Petticoat, Record Mirror* (as *Record and Radio Mirror* from September '73), *Romeo, Sounds, Valentine*; with very special thanks to the archives of Tom Sheehan.

Counterculture/adult/gay and women's lib: *Gay News, International Times, Rock'n'Roll Madness Funnies, Spare Rib, Time Out.*

American publications: *Billboard, Cashbox, Creem, Los Angeles Times, New York Times, New Yorker, Rolling Stone, Star* (February to June '73), *TV Guide, Variety, Village Voice.*

For extra help and facilitating, many thanks to Max Bell for Biba memories, Mark Blake and Dave Lewis for trying to help locate that old cinema, Tom Doyle for period Dundee specifics, Natalie Jones at Reach PLC and Neil Raj at The British Library.

BOWIE**IMAGES**73

FRONT COVER
'Who'll love Aladdin Sane?' (Paperback © Masayoshi Sukita; Hardback special edition © LWT/Shutterstock).

IMAGES page 1
Lonely planet boy. David in the Smoking Lounge at Radio City Music Hall, New York, 14 February 1973 (© Masayoshi Sukita).

IMAGES pages 2–3
Top row: 'See you, Ziggy!' David about to board his train to Bonnie Scotland, 15 May 1973 (© John Glanvill/AP/Shutterstock); 'Nice one, Vera!' Veruschka models Tonik by Dormeuil, 'The mohair for men' (© Bettmann/Getty Images); Björn gives his 'Weenyborgers' something to shriek about (© Paul Popper/Popperfoto/Getty Images); The newly shorn 'street punk' Marc in October '73 – in one of his more transparent fibs he told *Valentine* magazine his haircut was given to him by his 'very good friend' David Bowie (© Koh Hasebe/Shinko Music/Getty Images).
Bottom row: The people's noize – Wolverhampton wonders Slade (© Jorgen Angel/Redferns/Getty Images); A bloody casualty of the IRA's first mainland bombing of the Seventies outside London's Old Bailey, 8 March 1973 (© David Cairns/Hulton Archive/Getty Images); A loyal subject (© Evening Standard/Hulton Royals Collection/Getty Images); 'ChinniChapp' golden boys The Sweet (© Jorgen Angel/Redferns/Getty Images).

IMAGES pages 4–5
The freakiest show: David's apostles arouse police suspicion outside Hammersmith Odeon as they unknowingly await Ziggy's final stand, 3 July 1973 (© Peter Stone/Mirrorpix).

IMAGES pages 6-7
The Husband (left-hand side): Mr Jones in his 'Sorrow' suit for *The 1980 Floor Show*, 18 October 1973 (© Michael Ochs Archives/Getty Images).
The Wife (right-hand side): The indispensable Mrs Jones looks the other way at King's Cross station, 15 May 1973 (© Evening Standard/ Hulton Archive/Getty Images).
The Lovers (middle panels, clockwise from top left): Amanda Lear plays 'Dooshenka' in *The 1980 Floor Show*; when it aired, one reviewer mistook her for Veruschka – more worryingly, the *Village Voice* thought she was Wayne County (© NBC Universal/Getty Images); Pearly queen Marianne Faithfull with her Ricci Burns crop (© Evening Standard/ Hulton Archive/Getty Images); Mad about the house, Ava Cherry (© NBC Universal/Getty Images); Fanny girl Jean Millington (© Ian Dickson/Redferns/Getty Images).

IMAGES page 8
'Heavens to Murgatroyd!' David gets Snagglepussed by fans on his return to Charing Cross, 4 May 1973 (© Mike Lloyd/Mirrorpix).

ENDPAPERS
The seat with the clearest view, Radio City Music Hall, 14 February 1973 (© Masayoshi Sukita).

Picture research and layout concept by Simon Goddard.

THANKYOU

A special arigatō to Aki Sukita.

The glossy pin ups of Omnibus Press: David Barraclough, Claire Browne, Greg Morton, David Stock and the great northern Debra Geddes of Great Northern PR.

For their valued support: Mike Scott, Francis and Martin in Cardiff, Mark in Walthamstow and the legendary Tony Linkin (The David Bowie Fan Club membership number 2250: joined April 1973).

For battle cries and champagne: Kevin Pocklington at the North Literary Agency and braw boppin' copy-editor Alison Rae.

And to Sylv – twenty years and counting with a lad insane.

DAVID BOWIE
will return in

BOWIEODYSSEY74

COMING 2024